LIVING
THROUGH THE
RACKET

Hay House Titles of Related Interest

LIVING
THROUGH THE
RACKET

How I Survived Leukemia . . .
and Rediscovered My Self

Corina Morariu

with Allen Rucker

HAY HOUSE, INC.
Carlsbad, California • New York City
London • Sydney • Johannesburg
Vancouver • Hong Kong • New Delhi

Published and distributed in the United States by: Hay House, Inc.: www.hayhouse
.com • *Published and distributed in Australia by:* Hay House Australia Pty. Ltd.: www
.hayhouse.com.au • *Published and distributed in the United Kingdom by:* Hay House
UK, Ltd.: www.hayhouse.co.uk • *Published and distributed in the Republic of South
Africa by:* Hay House SA (Pty), Ltd.: www.hayhouse.co.za • *Distributed in Canada by:*
Raincoast: www.raincoast.com • *Published in India by:* Hay House Publishers India:
www.hayhouse.co.in

Editorial supervision: Jill Kramer • *Project editor:* Shannon Littrell
Design: Riann Bender
Interior photos courtesy of the author, except where noted

Library of Congress Cataloging-in-Publication Data

Morariu, Corina.
   Living through the racket : how I survived leukemia-- and rediscovered my self /
Corina Morariu.
      p. cm.
   ISBN 978-1-4019-2649-6 (tradepaper : alk. paper) 1. Morariu, Corina. 2. Tennis
players--United States--Biography. 3. Women tennis players--United States--
Biography. 4. Leukemia--Patients--United States--Biography. I. Title.
   GV994.N38M67 2010
   796.342092--dc22
   [B]
                                     2009038812

ISBN: 978-1-4019-2649-6

13 12 11 10   4 3 2 1
1st edition, February 2010

Printed in the United States of America

To Collin and Chet

CONTENTS

FOREWORD

by Billie Jean King

You never really appreciate someone's character until it is truly revealed. For years I have known that Corina is intelligent, knowledgeable, and fun. But through her struggle, I also learned that she is a special person and has really earned her badge of courage.

Corina and I will forever be connected through the most emotional and competitive event in my coaching career. She was part of the 1998 United States Fed Cup team (international team play for women) that I coached. We had a formidable opponent in the team from Spain—playing in Madrid. It was July 1998; and Corina, Monica Seles, Lisa Raymond, and Mary Joe Fernandez were brought to the Club de Campo Villa de Madrid to take on Conchita Martinez, Arantxa Sanchez-Vicario, Magui Serna, and Virginia Ruano Pascual in the Fed Cup semifinals.

Looking back, the amazing thing about that Fed Cup (or matchup between nations) was that Corina did not hit a ball in competition that week. But she was the glue that held our team together. She gave the players strength. Her insight helped me be a stronger coach. And she was just as important—and played just as big a role—as any member of the team. It was in Madrid that I really got to know Corina and saw what an inspiration she is. Not all that much later, everyone would see the true depth of Corina's positive attitude and willpower. We saw the essence of this woman not on a tennis court, but in a hospital room.

Coming from a family of doctors, Corina had become so accustomed to the medical terminology you would have thought she'd spent her days practicing medicine instead of hitting tennis balls. I remember visiting her near the end of 2001 at Jackson Memorial Hospital in Miami at the peak of her battle with leukemia. She was wearing a bandana, and her hair was gone. There was a portal in her neck. She had lost weight, and nothing good was happening. Yet despite all of these challenges looming over her, she was so positive. I was thinking, *I may never see this woman again,* but through it all, she maintained her cheerfulness, great outlook on life, and strong will to beat this beast that had put her in a corner.

Corina's journey to good health was a long and challenging one. She had several grueling rounds of chemotherapy—each taking a bite out of her physically and emotionally—but she was up for the fight. And she not only got better, she pulled through and fought hard to return to the levels of life she enjoyed and expected. Just 16 months after she began this life-changing ordeal, she was back on the tennis court. Believe it nor not, she was once again playing on the WTA (Women's Tennis Association) Tour.

Corina is a real champion in every sense of the word. During her career she won one WTA Tour title, and also won the top prize at a handful of ITF (International Tennis Federation) events, but she really excelled at my favorite part of tennis: doubles. Throughout the years that she played on the Tour, she won 13 doubles tournaments, including two major titles: the 1999 Wimbledon women's doubles (with her good friend Lindsay Davenport), and the 2001 mixed doubles at the Australian Open (with Ellis Ferreira). After her illness, Corina came back to the sport (and to her friends) and played exceptionally well. She returned with the class and courage that defines who she is as a human being. That fighter mentality is always there with Corina. You notice it on the tennis court, and you appreciate it when you spend time with her.

Many of us have been blessed to lead wonderful lives, but when we look at women and men who have won the types of battles Corina has waged, we understand that the combination of a powerful human spirit and positive thinking is a strong attribute in anyone, but in a person like Corina Morariu, it is a lifesaver.

• • • • • •

FOREWORD

by Lindsay Davenport

I can't recall the first time I encountered Corina on the women's tennis Tour, but I vividly remember the first time I played doubles against her. It was at a tournament in Florida in 1997, and I was playing with my then partner, Mary Joe Fernandez. We were on top of the doubles world at the time, having won the ITF Doubles Championship title the year before; while Corina, who turned pro in 1996, and her partner, Angela Lettiere, were fresh-faced newcomers. In any case, when Mary Joe and I walked out on the court, the stands were filled to the rafters. We were both a little embarrassed, thinking that everyone was there to watch *us*—but, as it turned out, they were all there to watch Corina and Angela! Those two had packed the house with friends from all over Florida. Mary Joe and I were flabbergasted. We were the best in the world, but the whole crowd was on *their* side!

Corina always had her fans (one pundit, for example, said that she was "known for a picture-perfect one-handed backhand and a sunny disposition"), and as I got to know her, I became one of her *biggest* fans. First of all, she's a lovely person, even when she's trying to knock a tennis ball down your throat. You can't say that about a lot of professional tennis players, unfortunately. Many are so self-centered and driven that they're only smiling when they're winning, and winning is only a sometimes thing, even with the best players in the world. Corina was someone you could like even if you were losing and she was winning. Her life was not just about tennis. She had the capacity, even at a young age, to see beyond the game.

But make no mistake: Corina was a great tennis player. My coach directed me toward her as a partner in 1999 because I was the #1 singles player in the world at the time and under tremendous pressure. I needed someone in doubles who would be good, but also fun and relaxing to play with. The very first time Corina and I played together, we won. And it wasn't at some warm-up tournament on a tropical island somewhere. It was Wimbledon! I had just beaten the great Steffi Graf to win the singles title—and I guess the fact that I was so loose and almost floating and Corina was so good (or maybe too scared to screw up), helped us play as if we'd played together for years. I remember it was such a crazy, surreal moment when it was all over. I realized that not only had I found a great partner, I'd found a great friend.

Corina has faced tremendous struggles in her life, both on and off the court, and I am here to attest that she has dealt with most of them like a true champion. In 2000 she became the #1 doubles player in the world, and exactly one year after our Wimbledon victory—and a slew of other wins in between—she broke her elbow on the court in the opening singles round of Wimbledon. And I was her opponent! Then she'd barely gotten back on her feet as a player when she was diagnosed with leukemia. I will never forget seeing her for the first time in the hospital in Miami. Here was one of the healthiest, most athletic people I've ever met looking frail, thin, and ashen, battling for her life. It was emotionally very tough for me to see her like that. I can't imagine what it must have been like for *her.*

But, as you will read, she came back. She didn't just survive; she thrived. Before anyone would have predicted, she was back on the Tour. Then she had severe shoulder problems. And came back again. Then she was in a terrible car wreck. And came back again. Before it was all over, she and I made it to the finals of the Australian Open and won a title in Bali together. And I had a sister for life.

I can't really say how the leukemia changed Corina (I'll let her explain that), but I *can* say that the person I became so close to afterward is one of the most resilient, tough-minded, independent women I have ever met. In tennis, you lose a lot, but you learn to win by losing. Even so, I could never imagine that someone could get cancer, lose so much in the process, and yet come back and reinvent her whole life so that she is now healthier in every way than before she got sick. I mean, I never could have imagined that *before* I had the distinct pleasure and honor of knowing my friend—and in many ways, my inspiration—Corina Morariu.

• • •   • • •

INTRODUCTION

I started playing competitive tennis when I was six years old, urged on by my father. And on April 3, 2000, at the age of 22, I achieved something I had only dreamed of.

A few weeks before, my dear friend and frequent doubles partner Lindsay Davenport and I had won the title at the annual WTA tournament in Indian Wells, California, just south of Palm Springs. We beat Martina Hingis and Mary Pierce, two world-class champions, in the semifinals, and then Anna Kournikova and Elena Likhovtseva in the finals. In addition, I made it to the third round in the singles competition, singles being my main focus at the time. Walking back to the parking lot after the doubles victory, I remember turning to my husband, Andrew (who was also my coach at the time), and announcing, "I am really happy right now."

April 3 was a Monday, and I was back home in Boca Raton, Florida, practicing for the next tournament on the WTA Tour. The world tennis rankings come out every Monday, and these rankings are the cold, hard, indisputable representation of how well you've been playing, how you're regarded by other players and the press, and where you'll be seeded in the next tournament. The system is calculated by numbers, and the numbers don't lie. It's a set ritual for many pro players to check the new rankings every Monday morning to see where they stand. To some, it's more than a measure of achievement. It's a measure of self-worth.

After a difficult Monday-morning practice, I went online to see where I was ranked. I'd won the Wimbledon doubles title with Lindsay the year before, and my doubles ranking had steadily improved from a position in the high 20s. I was anticipating good news, and I got it. There, in the women's doubles column, was my name in the very first slot.

I was, at that moment, the #1 women's doubles player in the world.

I didn't start jumping up and down or become outwardly excited. I didn't plan a huge party or break open a bottle of Cristal. I just did what was customary for me: got in the shower to clean up after practice. But everything *was* different. I stood there in that stream of warm water and smiled as a wave of satisfaction washed over me. *I was the #1 doubles player in the world,* and even though singles was my priority at the time, I still felt a tremendous sense of accomplishment. I let myself thoroughly enjoy the moment, fully cognizant of the years and years of hard work, sacrifice, and emotional trauma that it had taken to reach this benchmark.

I had played or practiced tennis virtually every weekday and most weekends since I could remember. On endless Friday afternoons as a kid, when all of my schoolmates were planning a weekend of fun, I was preparing to travel to an age-appropriate tennis tournament somewhere. By the eighth grade, I was waking up at 5 A.M. every day to go to the gym to work out before heading to school—then I'd go from school to an afternoon practice, and straight home for dinner and homework. In high school, we arranged for my classes to start at 9:30 so that I could complete a long practice before class each day while still maintaining the same afternoon schedule. I played on my high-school tennis team, which was genuinely fun, but I was also out of town much of that period playing on the very competitive, under-18 International Junior Tennis Tour. Let me tell you, it severely cuts into your adolescent social life when you have to go to a tournament in

Australia or a satellite pro tournament in Tunisia instead of the Friday-night varsity football game.

By age 22—having skipped college to continue my climb up the pro ranks—I was accustomed to this life, and it was now paying off. The #1 ranking was the culmination of a nine-month winning streak through which I'd won four tournaments with Lindsay, including Wimbledon, and one more with my friend Kim Po. I had also won my first singles title the year before and saw myself constantly improving as a singles player. If you had asked me on that Monday how I saw my future, I would have said that I had my work cut out for me in trying to hold on to the #1 doubles ranking while also striving to advance my singles ranking. However, I was still young, gaining valuable experience and continually improving. I truly thought that my best tennis years were yet to come.

It didn't quite work out that way, which is why you're reading this book. The day I attained the #1 spot was incredible, but it now seems like a lifetime ago. Sure, I was living a dream existence, as I traveled the world in the rarefied circles of the professional tennis player, but my life was about to be turned completely upside down. It would take years before I could make sense of the inevitable fallout.

As you probably guessed from the title of the book, I contracted cancer.

A devastating illness has a way of upending anyone's life, especially one like mine, which was so structured; disciplined; and, in many ways, one-dimensional. It can undermine everything you count on and set you off in directions, good and bad, that you never really contemplated before. Although my personal identity had been deeply intertwined with my tennis identity for most of my first 23 years, much of what occurred in the wake of my illness was only tangentially related to tennis. It was much more connected to my view of myself as a person and how I came to define my life, on my own terms. The greatest change came through my most personal relationships, the details of which I have laid out as honestly as I can. The cancer was the catalyst, but the relationships were the real crucibles for growth.

I had been tested during my entire life—in fact, every time I walked onto a tennis court in competition—but I had never been tested like this.

LIVING THROUGH THE RACKET

Most of us think of suffering as just that: suffering. Yet as I came to learn, some forms of suffering can present an opportunity for personal transformation borne of the obvious and inescapable pain, anguish, and sadness experienced by both ourselves and the people who love us most. We certainly don't invite disease or any other form of suffering into our existence, but it is part of life, and once confronted by it, there is no way to predict how we might change. In my case, the changes that occurred made life better, richer, and more meaningful in so many ways.

• • •   • • •

Chapter 1

OUT OF BODY

A tennis player's life is measured in tour dates on a yearly schedule beginning in January—leading up to the Australian Open—and ending sometime in November, depending on which tournaments you choose to play after the U.S. Open finishes in mid-September. The six or so weeks you have off after that are usually devoted to a rigorous training schedule spent preparing for the next season, which begins after New Year's. In the prime of a professional career, there is little time to do anything else. You're either playing, practicing, training, or traveling.

At the beginning of the WTA Tour season in 2001, I was in excellent shape, eager to begin the year. I was coming off several tough months, though. After being ranked #1 in women's doubles in April 2000, I literally stumbled and took a big fall. In my opening singles round at Wimbledon, I had the misfortune of being pitted against my good friend Lindsay, who also happened to be the defending champion and the #1 ranked singles player in the world. In the second game of the second set, already down one set, I made an abrupt change of direction, slipped on the damp grass court, and broke my left arm at the elbow. I let out a bloodcurdling scream when I hit the surface, and Lindsay came running to help. A picture of her leaning over my crumpled body made newspapers around the world. It was a painful moment in many ways.

I walked off Centre Court with this lifeless arm, and it would be four months before I could compete again. Lindsay and I couldn't defend our Wimbledon doubles title, and I ended up missing the U.S. Open as well. I finally returned to competition in October at a tournament in Tokyo, right near the end of the Tour season. Half of the year 2000, in other words, was a washout.

I trained especially hard in the off-season, got into the best shape possible, found my rhythm again, and was set for a mini-comeback. I started the season at a tournament in Sydney, a traditional warm-up to the Australian Open, and made the quarterfinals of the singles. I beat Anna Kournikova, ranked 8th in the world at the time, and did it decisively (6-2, 6-1) in a quick 46-minute match. I went on to the Australian Open, full of hope and bolstered by confidence . . . and completely choked in my first round in singles. Losing in tennis is a constant—no one wins every tournament—but this loss particularly hurt because my expectations were so high.

But all was not lost, since I was back playing doubles with Lindsay at the Australian. We'd both had our share of injuries over the years, which prevented us from playing together as much as we wanted. But here we were, back to our winning form and making it to the finals, my first Grand Slam final since winning Wimbledon in 1999. On my 23rd birthday, after being up 3-1, we lost to the Williams sisters, Venus and Serena, 6-4 in the third set. It was heartbreaking to be so close to another Grand Slam title.

Fortunately, my tournament wasn't finished. I had teamed up with South African–born Ellis Ferreira at the Australian to play mixed doubles. Two days after losing the women's doubles title, Ellis and I won the mixed-doubles title, beating Joshua Eagle and Barbara Schett, 6-1, 6-3. I told the press that it was "a belated birthday present." It was the only mixed-doubles title of my career. Ellis and I had planned to play, and hopefully win, many more, but other things got in the way.

I was off to an excellent start: one Grand Slam title, one Grand Slam final, and a strong singles statement in beating Anna Kournikova in Sydney. In March, I went to California to play at Indian Wells, one of my favorite stops on the Tour. I had just come off a good week in Acapulco, and I was really looking forward to going to the desert, especially since I'd played well there in years past. In my last match at Indian Wells the year before, I'd won the doubles title with Lindsay. Feeling confident after my performances early in the year, I thought I was in for a good week.

I was ranked around 30 in singles at the time, and my first-round opponent was Nicole Pratt, who was ranked considerably lower. She was a scrappy, tenacious player, but I had never lost to her, so I thought this was a good opening-round matchup for me. We were scheduled to play first on stadium court, but the match was over before it began. I lost badly, 6-3, 6-1.

I still have trouble describing the strange feeling I had on the court that day. I felt like I was watching myself from outside the stadium, as if I were having an out-of-body experience (but not in a good way). I couldn't concentrate, my mind was foggy and unfocused, and I felt apathetic about the outcome of the match.

I blamed fatigue, along with something I often tried to ignore, especially when I was winning: my on-again, off-again dissatisfaction with my career choice.

ALTHOUGH I'D JUST TURNED 23, I'D BEEN PLAYING TENNIS almost constantly for much of my life. I started at the age of 6, beginning with local tournaments in Florida, progressing to international Junior tournaments, and eventually turning pro at 18. I never felt that tennis was the be-all and end-all of my existence, and I never had an innate love for the game. My father pushed me to play when I was very young, and there were times growing up when I felt that I was living *his* dream, not mine. However, with his urging, I worked exceedingly hard to improve my game. I ended up being better than I expected, and probably even better than *he* expected. By the time I realized I might want to do something else with my life, I'd already invested so much time and effort in tennis that I figured I owed it to myself to see how far I could go.

There were definitely parts of playing the game that I loved, but there were also parts I hated, and ironically, the two were often intertwined. I loved the lifestyle, I loved being my own boss and making my own schedule, and I loved the financial rewards. Most of all, I loved seeing my hard work pay off. Tennis, unlike most things in life, is very black-and-white. You win or you lose. You have a number next to your name (your ranking) that clearly defines where you stand in relation to everyone else. If you want to gauge your results, the rewards for all of your efforts, there is nothing more tangible than that. Yes, sometimes luck doesn't go your way, or you just end up losing to a better player. Even so, I knew that if I worked hard and put forth my best effort on the court, the results would eventually pay off. And they did.

At the same time, I hated the pressure, as well as the person I became when dealing with it. Before or during tournaments, the stress and tension of being measured so definitively by results would weigh on me, and I'd become edgy or downright cranky. After a tough loss, I'd often get depressed or withdrawn, spending sleepless nights replaying costly mistakes in my mind. Part of the beauty of tennis—the one-on-one aspect—is also what makes the sport so agonizing. I struggled with the idea that two people could take the court on any given day, one wins and one loses, and they each go home feeling good or bad about themselves accordingly. I was constantly trying to weather the emotional highs and lows.

Because of this love-hate relationship with the game, I always said that I didn't want to play professionally for an extended period of time. On the Tour, a player has to play a certain number of tournaments at a certain level for five years to acquire a financial pension. My plan was to fulfill my five-year obligation and then reevaluate things. Considering that at the time of Indian Wells, I was about four and a half years in, I was in the process of reevaluating already. Looking back, my retirement plan was also a way for me to alleviate the pressure, especially when things weren't going well.

My poor play and apathy at Indian Wells had nothing to do with my general health, at least in my own mind. It simply struck me as a sign that maybe my tennis days were numbered, and I was ready to move on and try something else. I had no other explanation. It was unlike me not to give 100 percent. I worked exceedingly hard, and I took pride in playing professional tennis—I was always determined to do it to the best of my ability. My performance at Indian Wells was out of character, but I figured I was losing my edge. I decided to play out the season (that is, fulfill my pension requirement) and then change course.

I lost in the quarterfinals of the doubles at Indian Wells, playing with Lindsay, and decided to take the next week off and skip one of the biggest tournaments of the year in Miami. I'd never played well there, and even though it was close to my home in Boca Raton, I chose instead to go to Park City, Utah, to decompress and regroup for the rest of the season.

Professional tennis, like most pro sports, is physically and mentally grueling. In a touring season of more than 40 weeks, you can play in excess of 22 tournaments, including the 4 major Grand Slams (the Australian Open, the French Open, Wimbledon, and the U.S. Open), while traveling to all parts of the world and racking up the frequent-flier miles. Even in peak condition and the best possible mind-set, it can at times sap both your energy and enthusiasm for the game. You may even start to wonder why you play.

I CAME TO TENNIS THROUGH MY FATHER, ALBIN. My dad emigrated to America from his native Romania and built a rich, productive life as a neurologist through an indomitable will and an unwavering desire to succeed. My mother, Rodica, who was also a physician in Romania, possesses the same fortitude and courage.

I see myself very much as the child of immigrants, the product of two distinctly different cultures. Although I was born in America, my parents saw the world through their upbringing in Eastern Europe. My success in professional tennis, and my brother's success in amateur tennis, then academics, and ultimately in medicine, is the direct result of our parents instilling us with a strong work ethic and the mandate to succeed.

When my father was 33, Romania was being ruled by the Communist dictator Nicolae Ceaușescu. Although he was a successful doctor, my dad made the decision to leave his native country. Smuggling some of his scientific research to America, he landed a job in Minneapolis, but the Romanian government refused to issue him a passport. His opportunity finally came when he successfully treated a Communist official, who returned the favor by granting him a passport. However, the government would not issue one to my mom or my brother,

Mircea, who was four at the time. They wanted to keep my father's wife and child in the country as insurance that he would come back.

Dad took off for America on his own without telling a soul—not his parents, not his colleagues, not his wife—that he never intended to come back. He didn't even take his medical diploma for fear that a customs official would find it and not let him leave. He left Romania with the equivalent of ten U.S. dollars in his pocket and the hope of a better life.

My father lived alone in Minneapolis for three years, walking to work at the hospital every day from a bare-bones studio apartment. During that time, he couldn't communicate openly with his family in Romania because the Communist government liked to tap phone lines and open mail. He eventually made enough money to bribe the government to let my mother and brother leave. They finally made it to the U.S. in 1975.

Life in the States was a terrible struggle for my mom. Barely speaking English, she couldn't practice medicine, and she was extremely attached to her family and a culture that she would likely never see again. She might as well have been on another planet, and every day brought tears. She learned English by watching soap operas, and finding her way around a grocery store was a major ordeal. Mircea, now seven, was forced to make adjustments to his new life as well, although not all of them were painful. In Romania, bananas were rare and only available once a year. My brother tried to prolong the supply as long as he could and ate them in any color—green, yellow, or brown. In the States, bananas were plentiful, and Mircea, in heaven, ate a bunch daily. He "overdosed" after nearly a year of banana engorgement. To this day, he'll jokingly tell you that he can't get near a banana.

Eventually, my father landed a better job as a staff neurologist at Henry Ford Hospital in Detroit, so he moved the family there. My dad was doing everything in his power to create a better life, but my mother was lonely and plagued by homesickness. At one point, things became so strained that my mom nearly left my dad to return to Romania. Then, at age 39, she unexpectedly became pregnant with me and things changed. My father always says that she was completely cured of her depression the minute she found out she was pregnant.

I grounded her in this new world, and in a way, we learned how to adjust to life together.

MY ATHLETIC GENES COME FROM MY FATHER'S FATHER. Fiercely patriotic, my grandfather was devastated when his son left his family and his beloved country to pursue his dream in America. My grandfather died in 1974, while my father was in Minneapolis. My dad couldn't even go back for his own father's funeral; if he returned, he would never get out again. My grandfather was an engineer by trade, but his greatest accomplishment was having been a champion gymnast. For at least five years in his youth, he was one of the best gymnasts in Romania, a country that later produced the legendary Nadia Comaneci and Bela Karolyi. He had the opportunity to represent Romania at the Summer Olympics in Los Angeles in 1932, but couldn't raise enough money to make the trip. He later competed against, and defeated, the Olympic champion.

In Romania, the father is the final arbiter of all things. My grandfather told my father that he was to do two things: go into medicine and learn to play either tennis or volleyball. My grandfather didn't want his son to go into gymnastics because of possible injury, and soccer was also deemed too dangerous. My dad chose tennis because it was an individual sport and, in his words, "I had my destiny in my own hands."

It's funny: My dad did exactly what his father told him, without question, until he reached his 30s. Then he turned his back on everything his father cherished—family, country, and culture—to set out on his own. Nevertheless, Dad never seemed to question the role of parent as the ultimate authority when it came to his own kids. That was the legacy of his immigrant past and the engine for my tennis career.

My father continued to play tennis after coming to America. He played with and taught my older brother, and then he started me in the sport when I was two. Playing regularly at a local club in Detroit, he'd always take me along. I loved the social aspect of those outings. The women at the front desk would prop me up on the counter, and I would talk to everyone. Social butterfly that I was, I enjoyed being the center of attention. After my dad had finished playing, he'd give me a racquetball racket and hit balls with me. One day, so the story goes, he came home from work and decided not to play tennis. Apparently, I went ballistic, and my father took this to mean that I loved tennis and wanted to play more. Looking back, however, I see that I was probably more disappointed at missing out on my social hour. Regardless, my tantrum more or less sealed my fate at age two-and-a-half. My dad didn't decide to be a doctor (his dad did), and I didn't really decide to be a tennis player—it was decided for me. Soon after that, we moved to Florida, and I played my first tournament there when I was six.

I KNOW MY DAD ALWAYS HAD MY BEST INTERESTS AT HEART. He never thought he was too pushy or too pressuring like many obsessed tennis parents are, but I felt differently. He has a very forceful, mercurial personality; and memories of my early tennis life are stressful.

On my desk, I have a photo of me as a six-year-old getting ready to play my first tennis tournament. I have the whole getup—skirt, headband, wristbands, racket bag—but when I look at that picture, I see a scared little girl about to throw up from fear. I was so nervous that I couldn't eat breakfast. I didn't know how to keep score, I was playing a girl a foot taller than I was, and my dad was breathing down my neck. Despite all that, I acquitted myself pretty well on the court. The more I played, the better I got . . . but for me, tennis was never purely fun.

My dad, of course, saw it from his perspective, not mine, and all the signs showed that I could be a very accomplished player. He wanted to pass on his own character strengths of dedication and discipline, which were obvious in his courageous act of coming to America alone and building a new life, and I certainly inherited those traits. If you ask him today what kind of pupil I was, he'd say, "She was very disciplined on the court, very articulate, and if you told her something she should do, she would do it. She was a kid who tried her best all the time. That's why she was good." As he later told me, "I just wanted you to be the best."

My dad had also introduced my brother to the game, and Mircea excelled at playing in the Juniors and ended up playing at the college level at Brown University. However, by the time I was playing tennis regularly, Dad was more established as a physician and had even more time to dedicate to coaching. "I improved on the first generation," is how he puts it. He also knew that fierce focus on an individual sport was a good way to keep us out of trouble and away from drugs. It worked. I've always stayed away from drugs (that is, if you don't count chemotherapy).

My dad was intense, and extremely dedicated to my development. He analyzed every match in great detail. Like many parents, only perhaps more forcefully, he never got around to telling me what I did right. Only after I complained bitterly about this did he decide to make two checklists: what I did wrong and what I did right. Still, after all these years, what stuck with me were his pointed and impassioned criticisms, sometimes coming at high volume.

When I was ten—a story my brother and I recount in detail to this day—I was playing a tournament and lost a close, hard-fought match in the third and final set, 6-4. It was an agonizing match, and surely I made some stupid mistakes (I was ten, after all) that contributed to my defeat. As we drove home after the match, I was in the backseat, and my dad was driving. Needless to say, he was unhappy with my performance. He was absolutely livid, screaming at me and banging on the steering wheel at the same time. At the height of his rage, he yelled at me, "You know what? You have the brain of a chicken!"

Straight from this devastating remark, he took me to a local track and made me run until he decided that I could stop. I got home and immediately called my brother, who was then away at college in Rhode Island. I was completely crushed and cried out to Mircea, "Dad just said I have the brain of a chicken!" And my brother broke out laughing. He thought it was the funniest thing he'd ever heard. I was shouting at him, "I can't believe you're laughing!"

"It's funny!" he managed to say, and he was right. To this day, my brother will randomly text me: "You have the brain of a chicken." As a matter of fact, he jokingly suggested that I call this book *Resurrection of the Brain of a Chicken.* The line gets a laugh every time.

My brother figured out by his midteens that he wasn't going to let our father rule his life—although, ironically, he did in time follow Dad's lead when it came to a career path. Not only did Mircea end up specializing in neurology like our father, but he also eventually went into practice with him. Still, at age 15, my brother announced that our dad could no longer be involved in his tennis, which really disappointed my father. So when *I* came along, Dad made up for it by getting completely, almost obsessively, involved in my game. I was the youngest, the baby girl, who was by nature a pleaser. I compulsively tried to become the perfect child. It seemed like the only thing I could control.

COMPARED TO SOME PARENTS I'VE ENCOUNTERED in my tennis life—parents who still breathe down their twentysomething prodigy's neck at major world tournaments and are overbearing, demanding, and borderline psychotic—my dad could be considered mellow, especially as I got older. He always had his own life and his own career, and he never looked to make a living off me. In fact, it was just the opposite: he was the one always supporting and providing for me. He was intense, but there was a reason behind it.

Tennis is such a highly technical sport that in order to master the skills involved, it's almost necessary to start playing for hours on end at a very early age. Rarely do you hear of a professional who started playing at age 11 or 12—most start at 6 or 7. And how many seven-year-olds want to spend every free minute practicing on a tennis court? Not many. They want to play soccer, lose themselves in video games, ride bikes, and have sleepovers. How many seven-year-olds want to make the commitment to excel at one thing unless they have a parent pushing them and essentially making that commitment for them?

The pressure and the stress were very tough on me. I distinctly remember waiting for my dad to pick me up from elementary school one Friday afternoon. We were off to one of the four or five statewide Junior tournaments that I had to play to get to the next big step, the Nationals. As school ended for the week, I was preparing for work—highly stressful work at that—while my friends were off to the movies and weekend sleepovers. I sat on that bench feeling anxious about the upcoming tournament, and at the same time, sad that I was missing out on old-fashioned childhood fun.

My life was by no means all stress and no joy, though. From sixth grade on, I went to a private prep school that accommodated my many trips, but staying in school was important to me because it brought normalcy to my life. I loved having friends who had nothing to do with, and knew nothing about, tennis. I also played high-school tennis for four seasons and thoroughly enjoyed it. I loved being on a team—it was a pleasant departure from the isolating existence that was becoming my life.

My parents are both incredibly loving, giving people; but my sweet, even-tempered mom was the counterbalance to my dad's drive and intensity. She could see the pressure I was often under and tried her best to alleviate it in any way possible. On the weekends when my dad was too occupied with work, my mom would take me to tournaments, and we enjoyed our trips together very much.

On one occasion, we arrived at a competition and realized that I'd forgotten to pack my rackets. We just started cracking up, and then we bought a racket at a local pro shop. I won the tournament, but we couldn't stop thinking about what would have happened if my dad had been along!

I'd often play poorly and walk off the court, dejected, to my mom clapping her hands and saying, "You played so well!" She had no real grasp of the intricacies of the game, but that was what I loved—she didn't care. She was simply thrilled to watch her children play.

By the time I was a teenager, my dad began to calm down and step back from my day-to-day tennis. Maybe if I had a different personality, I would have quit the game to pursue another kind of life. I knew deep down that I could walk away from tennis and my dad would love me regardless. But I rebelled in a different way. I became feistier. I had a coach at that time, but if my dad came to watch me practice and so much as uttered a word about my play, even something complimentary, balls would be hitting the back fence. I became as nutty toward him as he had been toward me. Genetics are a funny thing.

Even without his involvement, I only briefly thought about stopping. Tennis is a great parallel for life in that it requires discipline, a work ethic, determination, and strength through adversity. I knew I was developing skills that would serve me later in life, not just in tennis. Plus, by my midteens I'd already put in eight years of hard work, and the sport had seeped into my DNA. It also gave my father intense pride. He built a huge case—which my mom, brother, and I would later dub "the monstrosity"—to house my growing collection of trophies, perched alongside his own early trophies, my brother's, and the ones he and my brother had won together in father-son tournaments.

I dreaded the day the subject of a father-daughter tournament might come up.

No matter what my often-conflicted feelings about tennis were, on some level I didn't want to disappoint my dad. I wanted to be a success in his eyes and in my own as well. As Mircea later explained it, "It was just the way the two of us were raised. Your drive wasn't really focused on tennis per se; it simply became the medium for your drive for accomplishment."

• • • • • •

Chapter 2

THE NEWS

I came home to Florida after my short vacation in Park City in 2001 with a terrible cold, one that would take me weeks to recover from. I had also experienced a few nosebleeds in the weeks following my return, something that struck me as odd, if not alarming. My maternal grandmother in Romania had died of a virulent form of leukemia four years before, and I had the vivid recollection that some of her first symptoms were severe nosebleeds.

I went online to research nosebleeds and found that while they can be a symptom of leukemia, they can also accompany a common cold. I chastised myself for being a hypochondriac and never told anyone what was happening for fear of looking neurotic. Having both parents and a brother who were physicians, I'd learned over time not to complain about my health unless something major was wrong. A nasty cold and a couple of nosebleeds did not qualify as major, so I kept my mouth shut.

The cold lingered, but I recovered enough to put in some much-needed training and play my next scheduled tournament at Amelia Island, Florida, which is just north of Jacksonville. Again, I got my butt kicked in the opening round. This time my opponent was Rosanna de

Los Rios, and the score was a lopsided 6-3, 6-1. I wasn't plagued by the absentmindedness I had felt at Indian Wells, but I did feel totally outclassed on the court. This didn't bother me as much, since I'd tried hard and just lost to a better opponent on that day. Unlike the apathy I felt before, I was now determined to redouble my efforts and break this new first-round losing streak.

I played doubles with Mary Pierce, and the outcome was the same: another match, another loss. I used the time before the next tournament to practice even harder and spend more time in the gym, but I couldn't seem to get back into playing shape. My endurance was especially weak: I remember running on the treadmill one afternoon at six miles an hour, what should have been an easy pace, but I could barely keep myself upright. After 20 minutes, I was doubled over and heaving, unable to catch my breath and completely exhausted. I knew then that something was wrong. I called my dad, and we agreed that I should see a doctor when I got home. But neither of us thought it was anything more serious than the lingering effects of a persistent cold.

The next week took me to Charleston, South Carolina, and the lethargy I felt at Indian Wells returned. My husband, Andrew, wasn't with me that week, and with no one to push me to practice or work out, I had little desire to do either. I kept my practices to a minimum and concentrated more on enjoying the city with my friend Kim Po rather than trying to play world-class tennis.

There are incredible perks to being a professional tennis player, but the usual benefits of traveling rarely apply. You arrive at an event, and if you aren't practicing, playing, or working out, you're *waiting* to practice, play, or work out. There is a lot of waiting involved, and any time you might have away from the courts is usually spent resting in your hotel room.

Because I had so little energy for tennis, Kim and I decided to do some things we rarely did at tournaments: we took tours; had long, leisurely dinners; and just strolled around Charleston. We had a wonderful time together and came away from that trip with many fond memories. My memories of *playing* that week, however, are not so fond. I drew Meghann Shaugnessy, a young player quickly climbing up the rankings, in the first round. She was ranked well ahead of me and was having a great year, so I knew the match would be tough.

But since I'd never lost to her before, I thought I had a good chance. I got smoked, 6-3, 6-2, and continued my streak of not winning more than three games a set, let alone winning a first-round match.

The most staggering part of that match was my inability to concentrate. There are times in every match where concentration lapses, but an experienced player can recognize those lapses and stop them from spiraling out of control. I could do no such thing. I felt like I was in a vacuum. My physical energy was depleted, and to compound that, I couldn't get my mind to focus clearly. Tired and frustrated, I was ready to go home. (Home, for a nomadic professional athlete, usually cures all.) I had an appointment with a doctor and would hopefully get some help for the exhaustion that was now enveloping me. I was also going to have a week at home to reenergize, refocus, and prepare for the next leg of the Tour, which was a trip to Europe for a series of tournaments leading up to the French Open.

I went to see a pulmonary specialist, and after a series of tests, he concluded that my recent cold had exacerbated the effort-induced asthma I'd been diagnosed with ten years before. I hadn't had an asthma attack for three years, but he nevertheless prescribed an inhaler and sent me on my way. That was good enough for me. I was ready to resume work and prepare for the upcoming red-clay-court tournaments in Europe.

THE FIRST STOP ON WHAT I ANTICIPATED TO BE a nine-week European grind was in Bol, Croatia. I fell in love with Bol the first time I played a tournament there in 1997. Tennis players favor certain tournaments for different reasons: It could be the location; the food; the atmosphere; or, most likely, the results they've had at that particular event in years past. For me, Bol had all of the above. I reached my first-ever WTA Tour final there in 1997 and went on to make the final again the next year. The third year, I won the title.

Results aside, I fell in love with Bol's charm, beauty, and tranquility. It's a small town on the island of Brac, about an hour's boat ride from the mainland. The hotel we players stayed at was small but on the water, and it was walking distance from the courts. The stadium was intimate, the crowds were enthusiastic, and the tournament director took great care of us. And then there was the food.

As anyone who knows me will tell you, my life revolves around eating. I'm already thinking about lunch before breakfast is done, and I need to eat every three hours or people get hurt. It would only be fitting for me to judge a tournament by the culinary services they provide, and this event passed my test with flying colors. The tournament arranged for a restaurant in the hotel to be used exclusively by the players, their families, and their coaches, and all meals were provided there. I grew up eating Romanian food, and Croatian food is quite similar, so eating there felt like a taste of home.

While I was anxious to get to Bol for both the food and the atmosphere, I wanted to get back to winning, too. It didn't happen. I drew a feisty, highly ranked Japanese player named Ai Sugiyama in the first round, and I came out stumbling. I managed to get down 0-4 before she even broke a sweat. I recovered slightly, but lost the first set, 6-2. Then, by some miracle of will for which I'm still proud, I won the second set, 6-0. The momentum didn't last, however, and my concentration waned again. I lost the third set, 6-3. It was a tough loss to handle. I'd just lost in the first round of my favorite tournament, my fourth first-round loss in a row.

Tennis is a constant mental challenge. It is an individual sport in which one player must solely bear the burden and the responsibility of a loss. In fact, when it comes to tournaments, most of the players lose—some in the opening round, some later in the draw. Only 1 out of 32 or 64 or 128 actually walks away from that week without having lost a match. In order to keep playing in the face of such odds and not lose your sanity, you attempt to stay positive and persevere. It doesn't always work that way. The demons get the best of even the most talented players. In Bol, my positive spin was that I drew an especially tough opponent and won the second set without losing a game. That was progress, however small.

Losing four first rounds in a row is scary business for any pro, but off the court, things were becoming even scarier. My gums were bleeding, so much so that I woke up one morning with blood on my pillow. I chalked it up to gingivitis and dedicated myself to more brushing and flossing. I was winded when I ran, and my trusty little inhaler didn't seem to be helping. I developed pain in my right foot and went to see the trainer, who noticed bruises all over my body. I told her I bruise easily—I had an excuse for everything. As a tough professional athlete and the daughter of doctors, I wasn't about to complain about bleeding gums and bruises. So I headed to the next stop: Berlin.

There, things got worse. My foot pain went from moderate to severe, and after losing the first set of my first round to Marta Marrero, 7-5, I retired from the match. I pulled out of the doubles as well and stayed in Berlin to have my foot checked. Everyone thought I had a stress fracture, but both an MRI and a bone scan came up negative, leaving us all perplexed. It was two weeks before the French Open, and I had to make a decision: either stay in Europe, play through the pain, and hope that my foot improved with treatment; or go home and rest before the French. I decided to go home. That decision, it turned out, may have saved my life.

I GOT HOME ON A THURSDAY AND IMMEDIATELY HAD A BOOT, or a kind of walking cast, fitted for my foot to avoid weight bearing and speed the healing process. I also started going to my parents' office for treatment. They have a fully equipped facility with ultrasound machines and electronic muscle stimulator (stim) machines for pain management and rehab. I'd used this equipment often in the past to help recover from various injuries. My mother, who was in charge of many procedures in my dad's practice, administered these treatments. However, the first time she saw me in the office, she was shocked by my appearance—she thought I looked sick and kept asking me what was wrong.

My mom, like many mothers, tends to worry, so I tried to assure her that I was feeling fine. She insisted on taking blood, something else she could do right there in the office, and I went along, mainly to appease her. She attempted to find a vein, but couldn't. This seemed odd to both of us. Mom had taken my blood many times over the years and had never missed a vein. Yet I was getting annoyed at fruitlessly being stuck with a needle, so I convinced her to let it go.

That Friday, I woke up in the middle of the night because my nose had started to bleed. This didn't happen once or twice, but six or seven times over the course of a few hours. I mentioned it in passing to Andrew, but then let it go, again. In bed Saturday night, the same thing happened. I spent the better part of the night in the bathroom with tissues pressed to my nose.

I woke up on Sunday, Mother's Day, and my husband looked at me in horror—I was covered in bruises. My mom would later say that it looked as if someone had taken a baseball bat to me. Andrew was playing golf with my father that day and insisted that I let him tell Dad about the bruises and the nosebleeds. I reluctantly agreed, but told him not to make a big deal of it. I was still concerned about coming across as a whiner. My family had a nice Mother's Day dinner together that night, oblivious to the harrowing ordeal about to ensue.

The next morning, my dad told me that he'd made an appointment for me on Wednesday with a general practitioner, which was fine with me. Then he did something strange: he called me back a few hours later and said that he'd moved my appointment up to Tuesday, and I'd be seeing a hematologist, not a GP.

At that point, I didn't really care what kind of doctor I was going to see. What *did* bother me was that my father seemed worried, particularly since he tends to take most medical problems in stride. As I said, he came to the U.S. from Romania—alone, with no money, separated from my mom and brother for three years—to build a new life. He is a neurologist who deals regularly with incurable brain tumors and other deadly disorders, and is a tough guy by anyone's measure. The concern in his voice frightened me, but only briefly. The art of denial I'd obviously perfected kicked in, and I convinced myself that I was fine.

My dad would later say, "I didn't say anything, but I *was* worried. Your MRI was negative. We still put you in a protective boot because this is what you do with a stress fracture. What was happening, thinking retrospectively, is that all of your bone marrow was filled with malignant leukemia cells. That's why you were having foot problems."

The hematologist appointment was at 8:30 A.M. on Tuesday, May 15, 2001. I remember the date and time specifically because, as anyone who's ever been diagnosed with cancer or some other life-threatening illness can confirm, dates like this are forever etched in your memory.

I left Andrew sleeping and went to my appointment alone. The hematologist was Dr. Aurea Tomeski, a small, round Filipino woman who reminded me of my mom. She was extremely kind and gentle, and I had a good feeling about her from the start. I started to recount my recent medical history, and she stopped me at the nosebleeds.

"Are your gums bleeding?" she asked.

"Yes."

"Are you bruising?"

"Yes."

I remember wondering, *How does she know all this stuff?* That thought actually crossed my mind, as if she hadn't been practicing medicine since before I was born. She then told me that she was going to do some blood work and, depending on the results, possibly do some more tests. She didn't seem alarmed, so I remained calm, even after the nurse took my blood and the needle almost instantly left a bruise the size of a half-dollar on my arm.

After a few minutes, the nurse came in and told me that Dr. Tomeski wanted to see me in her office. *Uh-oh.* Immediately, I knew this was a bad sign. I started panicking as I followed the nurse into the office.

Before I even sat down, Dr. Tomeski announced, "Your blood work is abnormal." Then she said, "You are pancytopenic." *Pancytopenia* is the medical term for a pronounced reduction of white blood cells, red blood cells, and platelets, but at the time, I had no idea what the hell it meant. Looking back, it all made sense: I was having trouble concentrating and breathing because I didn't have enough red blood cells to carry oxygen to my brain and lungs. I was spontaneously bruising and bleeding because I didn't have enough platelets to clot my blood.

Dr. Tomeski then started to rattle off numbers, the first one being my platelet count, which was 29,000. Normal is between 150,000 and 450,000. She then told me that I'd have to have some more blood work and that I'd need a bone-marrow test. All I had ever heard about bone-marrow tests was that they hurt. Like hell.

I frantically asked the doctor what was wrong with me. She calmly laid out the possibilities: aplastic anemia, vitamin B_{12} deficiency, or . . . leukemia.

I was about to burst into tears at the mere mention of the word *leukemia.* Sitting there, alone and scared, I didn't know what to say or do. I finally asked her to call my father. I heard him pick up, and without even saying "Hello," he asked her, "Bad news?"

As Dr. Tomeski was talking to my dad, she held the paper with the results of my blood tests in front of her face so I couldn't see her expression. She was getting emotional. This, of course, freaked me out even more. I was trying with every fiber of my being not to cry hysterically. I later found out that Dr. Tomeski had a daughter exactly my age. I'm not sure if she was affected by diagnosing someone her daughter's age, by telling a father that his daughter might be dying, or both. I was comforted by her concern, but at the same time absolutely terrified by her response.

The doctor and my dad figured out the next round of tests while I sat there frozen, waiting to get out of that godforsaken place. After Dr. Tomeski handed me a prescription for more tests, I was out the door. I walked through the waiting room in a fog. I felt like I was in a dream, watching myself from afar, hoping I'd wake up from this nightmare.

I got to my car and finally burst into tears. I called Andrew and told him I might have leukemia. I was hysterical; I couldn't stop crying. I hung up and sat in my car wailing for what seemed like an eternity—I couldn't move or even breathe. I eventually composed myself long enough to drive to my parents' office. The first person I saw was my mom. Her eyes were red and swollen. I asked her if she'd been crying, and she said no. She asked me the same question, and I said no. We laughed and hugged, knowing we were both lying to bolster the other. Then Andrew walked in with the same puffy eyes. Clearly, he had not been crying either.

I then walked across the street to the local hospital for another blood test. The hematologist there reassured me that my problem was probably a virus that had entered my bone marrow, something that could easily be treated. I relaxed again, clinging to any shred of good news. After a few futile efforts on my left arm to draw blood, the nurse finally stuck me through the huge bruise already on my right arm and got the sample. Andrew and I went to lunch, then to the mall, in relatively good spirits. I am an avid shopper, so the mall was like therapy. I remember checking out a pair of pants, then looking at Andrew and joking, "Maybe we should wait to see if I'm going to live before buying these." He didn't think my joke was funny.

The next big step was the bone-marrow test. I was comfortable with Dr. Tomeski and wanted her to do it, but she wasn't available until the next day. I didn't mind waiting, but my father did. When he called me at home to tell me that he'd found another doctor who could do the procedure that afternoon, I lost it for the second time that day. Dad was trying to be helpful, but I saw his meddling as overbearing and controlling. Through my tears, I screamed that this situation was hard enough for me, and that I didn't need him getting involved and making things more difficult. Then I hung up on him. He called back five minutes later, apologizing profusely. Since my dad is not big on doling out apologies and I was the one acting crazy, this struck me as more odd behavior. I was relieved when he told me that he understood my feelings, and I could have things done the way I wanted.

I went to my office upstairs to research online just what exactly a bone-marrow test entailed. As I was reading about the difference between an aspirate and a biopsy—in an aspirate, they suck out the liquid part of the marrow; in a biopsy, they remove bone along with the marrow—my nose started to bleed again. Profusely. Blood was pouring out of my nose at an unbelievable pace, like an open faucet. I tried everything I could think of—pressure, ice, tissues—to get it to stop, or even slow down, but nothing worked.

Andrew finally rushed me back to my parents' office. They called Stella Tudoran, an ENT (ear, nose, and throat) specialist and a friend of the family, to help. She arrived with the necessary paraphernalia to stop the bleeding . . . but I had no idea what I was in for.

Thankfully, I didn't see the size of the packing that was violently shoved up my nostril, but I later learned that it was about the size of my middle finger, and that was exactly how it felt: as if someone had jammed their finger up my nose. The pain was excruciating, and the tears starting flowing immediately. There was a tremendous pressure in my head, something I can only compare to a brain freeze—but unlike that sensation, this one wasn't temporary. I'm not sure if I was in shock from the procedure or just generally terrified, but I began to shake uncontrollably, and I spent the next half hour convulsing in my parents' office.

I had to make one more trip across the street to the hospital to register for my bone-marrow test the following day. My dad had to transport me in a wheelchair, which under any other circumstance would have been cause for extreme protest on my part, but I was so ill and completely exhausted at that point that I didn't utter a single complaint.

As my dad would later put it: "You started to become sick. I mean, you were sick, sick, sick. I didn't know what was wrong with you. I knew you were weak, bleeding from the nose and other problems. But I had never seen a patient as sick as you were at that time."

We all decided that it would be best if I spent the night at my parents' house. It was an emotional evening spent talking to friends and informing them of my current state. I became increasingly weak and struggled all night with the finger-sized sponge lodged in my nostril. The pressure was so great that I found it difficult to open my eyes, yet the pain made it impossible to sleep. I spent the night hoping and praying that I didn't have cancer, and that this whole unbearable ordeal would be over soon.

THE NEXT MORNING, I ARRIVED AT THE HOSPITAL EARLY to get a platelet transfusion to ensure that my blood would clot during the bone-marrow test. This was indicative of how few functioning blood cells I had. Waiting for the test itself, surrounded by other patients getting transfusions and IV antibiotics, my fear amplified. The situation was becoming as much a mental and emotional ordeal as it was a physical one. How had I gone from playing a professional tennis tournament in Europe a week earlier to being transported in a wheelchair, waiting to have a needle jammed into my bone to determine what kind of disease was ravaging my body? Was I dying? Was this really happening?!

The bone marrow was going to be extracted from the back of my hip, so I curled up on my side in the fetal position, clutching two pillows. There were only three people in the room: the doctor, a nurse, and me. I felt completely alone, and the magnitude of what was happening finally started to sink in. I would have given anything at that point to have been facing someone familiar instead of a concrete wall, or to have my mom's hand to hold instead of two pillows.

Dr. Tomeski started the procedure, and I was unprepared for the violence of it. It never occurred to me that the needle doesn't just slide into the bone. The doctor started pushing and pulling, trying to get the needle to penetrate. When she finally succeeded, I felt a searing pain resonate through my entire lower body. I was praying for the procedure to end quickly, but there were problems. The doctor and the nurse began a frantic exchange in Filipino while I was awash in pain. After more pushing and shoving, the doctor removed the needle and announced that she couldn't get a good aspirate and had to take a biopsy. At least I knew what she was talking about—I'd done my research.

The process began again, and I wanted to beg them to stop but knew I couldn't. The biopsy, while even more painful than the aspirate, was vital to saving my life. Even so, it felt exactly like what they were doing: chipping off a piece of bone. Every fiber of my body felt like it was on fire. The only good news at that point was that I was no longer cursing the packing in my nose. When the procedure was finally finished, I was sore and in shock from the whole ordeal. I realized that not only had they taken a piece of me physically, but also emotionally. My innocence and naïveté were gone. I was fighting for my life, and I knew that things were never going to be the same.

I found out later that the problem my doctor encountered was that my bone marrow was so packed with cancer cells that it was impossible to get a good sample in an aspirate. At that time, of course, I had no idea what the biopsy would show, and wouldn't for another 24 hours. I spent the rest of the day at my parents' house nursing my sore hip. I was miserable. The pain from both the bone marrow and the packing was too much to take, so I finally persuaded my parents to have the packing removed from my nose. Dr. Tudoran came by, removed it, and the pressure was instantly relieved. It was the best part of that awful day.

Unfortunately, after a short walk to the kitchen to get something to eat, my nose started bleeding again. Dr. Tudoran improvised a modified packing that wouldn't be so uncomfortable—she placed a small amount of gauze in my nostril, then wrapped my nose with tape to secure the dressing—and told my mom to change the gauze regularly. The new problem was that while the gauze absorbed some of the blood from my nose, the excess was now dripping down the back of my throat. I spent most of that night spitting bloody saliva into a mug next to my bed. My mom, who is one of the kindest, gentlest people I have ever known, stayed with me the entire night. I needed her emotionally as much as I did physically. She got up religiously every hour to change the gauze, and while neither of us slept much, I think we both took solace in just being near each other.

The next morning, May 17, it took all the effort I could muster to cover the 20 feet from the bed to the bathroom. When I got back, I collapsed on the bed, out of breath. I was shocked by how weak and exhausted I was. My body was completely shutting down. I felt like I was dying.

Early that afternoon, Andrew was sitting at my bedside when my dad came in. With tears running down his face, he delivered the news.

I had acute promyelocytic leukemia.

• • •   • • •

Chapter 3

WELCOME TO CHEMO

I could barely pronounce "acute promyelocytic leukemia," let alone know what it meant, so my dad patiently explained everything to me.

Acute promyelocytic leukemia (APL) is one of eight subtypes of acute myelogenous leukemia (AML), a cancer of the blood and bone marrow. Seven of those subtypes have survival rates ranging from 20 to 40 percent. The other, APL, is the most treatable and has a survival rate of around 70 percent. The day before, my parents looked at my bone-marrow slides with a pathologist and found out that I had AML. It took another day to determine which subtype I had. They kept all information from me until they found out that I had the most benign form, APL.

My dad went on to tell me that the treatment for APL involved two kinds of chemotherapy, oral and intravenous, and I'd have to spend at least the next month in the hospital. He also said that he'd tried to hire a private plane to fly me to Seattle so I could be at one of the premier hospitals in the nation for treating leukemia, but then he changed his mind because he didn't think I could handle the trip. (I agreed—if I couldn't make it to the bathroom, there was no chance I was going to make it to Seattle.) He then exhausted all of his contacts in the South Florida area and found a doctor who could treat me at Jackson Memorial Hospital in Miami. This was great news, but there was one major problem: they didn't have any rooms available. I would have taken a broom closet at that point, but apparently that wasn't an option. Since I was obviously a critical case, all efforts were being made to find a room at Jackson immediately.

My reaction to this flood of information was both sadness and relief. The news was devastating, but at least I had a diagnosis. I'd known for days that something was seriously wrong, but the scariest part had been that I didn't know exactly *what* was wrong. I simply knew that my health was deteriorating at a rapid pace, and if I didn't get help, I was going to die.

Once the diagnosis was confirmed, the athlete in me took over. I now knew my opponent, and I had a strategy and a support team in place to defeat it. In an odd way, this was a familiar scenario. It was going to take will, conviction, perseverance, discipline, and a desire to win—skills I'd been honing since I was six years old.

No more than five minutes after this conversation with my dad, the phone rang. My new doctor, Mark Goodman, had miraculously found a room, and I could be admitted ASAP. Within an hour, my mom and Nino, a man who had worked as an assistant in my parents' office for years, loaded me in a wheelchair, placed me in the car, and drove the hour to Jackson Memorial.

Once we arrived, my mother went looking for a wheelchair while I waited in the car. Things had deteriorated so quickly that I could barely sit up, and I was anxious to get into the hospital just so I could collapse on a bed. I finally got to the admitting area, and as I was sitting there in my wheelchair, I started to feel self-conscious. Why were people staring? It suddenly occurred to me that I was a frightening sight. Ashen-faced and still wearing my pajamas, I had gauze secured to my nose with tape and was holding a tissue to soak up the blood that was leaking past the dressing. I was also petrified, since I'd never spent a night in the hospital, let alone a month. No wonder people couldn't look away from me.

I was eager to meet Dr. Goodman, and when he finally came by to introduce himself, the first thing he did was take my hand and say,

"You're going to be okay." At that moment, I completely understood why some doctors have a God complex. I instantly saw that my life was now in his hands—he might as well have been the Creator descending from on high to save me.

Yet as I was being wheeled to my room, I started panicking for a new set of reasons. I'm more than slightly embarrassed to admit that for a brief moment, the spoiled princess in me took over as I wondered what my room would look like. Would I have to share? The horror! But the real horror was the fear that my family would be forced to leave me every night, scared and alone, in this new, completely foreign environment.

When the nurse opened the door to room 1239, however, I felt as if I'd died and gone to heaven (okay, not a great cliché considering my condition). I'd been given the VIP suite, a spacious room with wood paneling, easy chairs, and an armoire with a TV and VCR. The best part about it was that I wouldn't have to be left alone. Family members could spend the night! Right away I got in bed and surveyed my new surroundings. I had an awful road ahead of me, but at least my hospital room helped me smile.

Meanwhile, my family was suffering, and coping, as well. My brother, Mircea, had been living in Boca Raton, after having completed medical school at the University of Miami and doing his residency at Georgetown University in Washington, D.C. But at the time I returned from Germany with my foot injury, he was on a mini-fellowship in Iowa. When my dad called him about my initial condition, he could only imagine two possibilities: aplastic anemia or leukemia. He was devastated, later telling me, "I just felt sick."

My brother and I are extremely close, probably as close as two siblings can be. He is ten years older than I am, and I've always looked up to him as my knight in shining armor. He was not only my protector growing up, but also my biggest supporter. Mircea would accompany me to national Junior tournaments around the country whenever he could. One summer when I was 14, he traveled to Europe with me for two weeks as my one-man support team. Those trips bonded us in a special way, and we have many cherished memories of the times we've spent together. My brother also makes me laugh like no one else can. Given the tough road I faced, I would need that now more than ever.

Mircea immediately made arrangements to fly home from Iowa. By this time he knew I had AML, but he didn't yet know that I had the more benign subtype, APL. He had to connect through Chicago and, as he says today, "I was sitting in O'Hare at one of the gates, and I was crying, just bawling. I think I looked kind of ridiculous to other people. I wasn't on the phone or anything—I was just crying."

While my mom and Nino were taking me to the hospital, Andrew had gone to pick up Mircea from the airport. The minute my brother got off the plane in West Palm Beach, he found out I had APL. He was so ecstatic that he was high-fiving perfect strangers.

I'd just gotten into bed at the hospital when he walked in the room with a big smile on his face and said, "Hi, cutie." He then followed that with something only my brother would say: "You won the leukemia jackpot!" As I was laughing, he handed me a present he'd picked up in the airport in Iowa. It was a little lamb wearing a sign that said I LOVE EWE.

Dr. Goodman then came in to explain the situation to Mircea, Andrew, Mom, and me. He spoke for 30 minutes at lightning-fast speed, and not always in complete sentences. Concentrating to understand him, we were like sponges trying to absorb the copious amounts of information flying at us. My mother, in particular, had a tough time understanding. After the doctor left, she looked at us with a pained expression and admitted, "I could barely understand anything he said." We had to laugh because she verbalized what all of us had been thinking. But we got the gist of the doctor's message: The road was going to be bumpy, and even life threatening at times. Yet he reiterated his assertion that in the end, I was going to be okay.

STRANGELY, I FELT COMFORTABLE AND ALMOST AT HOME that first night at Jackson Memorial. Andrew, Mircea, Mom, and I had dinner together that Thursday evening and watched the season finale of *Friends*, one of my favorite shows at the time. I still had the bloody nose and was hooked up to the IVs, which would be my constant companion for the next month, but a warm feeling of gratitude washed over me. I had a wonderful family, a great doctor, a decent prognosis, and a kick-ass suite. All things considered, I felt pretty damn lucky.

The next day, I was happily sedated as they took another bone-marrow sample from my hip to verify the initial diagnosis. Although

I never got a good look at it, my entire back was apparently bruised black from the two bone-marrow tests. Mircea, with his wry sense of humor, thought this could be useful: he'd ask people if they could interpret the Rorschach-blot appearance on my back, or if the interns and medical students would like to take a gander at the world's largest bruise. Cue the calliope music; I was like a sideshow at the circus.

The giant bruise was the least of my problems, though. First and foremost, my nose wouldn't stop bleeding. There were also times I'd get up to go to the bathroom and see that my sheets were covered in blood. I often had no idea where all the blood was coming from. Mircea and I finally traced the bleeding to the site of my bone-marrow test. When the intern came in to change the dressing, removing the bandage on my hip, blood began gushing—actually squirting—out. The intern started panicking, asking my brother to help stem the flow by pressing hard on my back, which of course, was already beyond sore. Mircea readily assisted, but recalls fighting back waves of nausea, even though he'd never been squeamish around blood. From all of his years of medical school and residency, he was accustomed to the sight of a lot of blood (and much worse), but seeing it streaming from his little sister's back was almost more than he could handle.

I started my oral chemotherapy on Friday, right after the diagnosis was confirmed. On Sunday night, I began the IV chemo, and I was very nervous. Despite all of the horror stories I'd heard about chemo, I had no idea what to expect. Mircea was holding my hand while the nurse found a vein in my bicep, because most of my other veins had collapsed at that point.

Within minutes of initiating the IV drip, I was experiencing major nausea. There were two plastic containers by my bed: one a small spit tray, the other a large basin. I told Mircea that I was going to throw up, and he handed me the spit tray. I immediately said, "Oh no, that's not going to cut it." He got a hold of the basin just in time—seconds later, I was spewing massive amounts of vomit. My body was completely rebelling against the poison being put into it. The explosion was so fast and powerful that I didn't even have time to feel bad about it. Welcome to chemo.

I QUICKLY REALIZED THAT A GOOD NIGHT'S SLEEP in the hospital was virtually impossible. Nurses would wake me up early to take blood, and the alarm connected to my IV would beep every few hours in the middle of the night. IV alarms have a very distinct three-tone ring, and in the days after I got out of the hospital, I swore I could hear it in my sleep. Compounding that, for reasons still unclear to me, the cleaning crew came in each day at 5 A.M. to take out the garbage, and they just *had* to turn all the lights on in the process. What happened to a peaceful night's sleep for cancer patients? The good news was: I wasn't going anywhere! I had the whole day to rest whenever I could.

My family went into divide-and-conquer mode, each member with a specific role. During the week, Mircea would stay with me, every day and night. (On the weekends, he'd go home to be with his wife, Laura, who was six months pregnant with their first baby.) He told my mom that he *had* to stay with me, that he wouldn't be able to live with himself if something happened to me while he wasn't there. He understood how sick I was. From the moment I'd left Germany, I was in danger of bleeding to death. Along with drastically reduced blood counts, another major complication of APL is spontaneous hemorrhaging, which I was clearly experiencing. But my cancer was so advanced that without provocation, I could also have bled internally—into my brain, lungs, or other organs.

My husband was also ever present and steadfast in his support. He set up an air mattress in the room that everyone in the family would take turns sleeping on. Andrew, along with Mircea, spent the most time with me in the hospital. Both of them continually brought food, magazines, and movies. And while they took care of anything I needed or wanted, it was their company that meant the most.

My brother and father were in private practice together, so Dad's role was to keep the business going, and he came to see me on weekends. I'm not a parent, but I often thought about how difficult it was for my mother and father to see me in the state I was in. It goes against the natural order of things. My dad, a big, strong man who saves lives for a living, had as tough a time as anyone. He threw himself into his work in an attempt to alleviate his anxiety over me, but when he was with me at the hospital, he couldn't hide his fear. Every time I would move or get up to go to the bathroom, he would anxiously tell my mom to help me. I finally had to say, "Dad, it's okay, I can handle it"—and I was referring to more than just my trip to the bathroom.

My mother, the glue of the family, did it all. She worked all day, helping my dad, and then she'd brave peak traffic to make the hour-long drive from Boca Raton to Miami. She later explained that no matter how exhausted she was, she felt as if she were being pulled by a magnet. She couldn't bear to be away.

Mom would try to find ways to make me feel better, even though just having her visit was enough for me. For example, she wanted to massage my calves every day. Half the time I was too tired or sick to care, but I always went along with it because it seemed to make her feel better. I think it gave her a sense of purpose and temporarily alleviated the helplessness she undoubtedly felt.

I'm sure my mother cried every time she drove to and from the hospital, but when she was in the room with me, she only did so once. She came in one day when I wasn't feeling well at all. I closed my eyes to rest, and after a few minutes, I could hear her sobbing uncontrollably. She must have thought that I was sleeping, so she could break down without upsetting me. I finally opened my eyes, put my hand on hers, and said, "Don't worry, Mom. I'm not going anywhere." She still says that was a moment she'll never forget.

There were days when I'd lie in that hospital bed with nothing to do but think, and my mind would wander. *What if I'm dying? What will my funeral be like?* I decided I wanted it to be a big party where everyone wore colorful clothes (black was forbidden); and where they'd celebrate, not mourn, the life I'd lived. It was weird, but I wasn't that scared of dying. Growing up, death had never been a taboo subject. My parents deal with it on a daily basis in their professional lives, and my family has always had a strong faith. I found peace in the belief that things happen the way they're supposed to. But don't get me wrong, I didn't *want* to die. I thought of all the things I hadn't been able to do yet and might *never* have the chance to do: go on safari, have kids, visit the Greek islands, meet my brother's baby. The list was endless. It wasn't the fear of dying that kept me going—it was my will to live.

ABOUT FIVE DAYS INTO MY STAY, I GOT A CALL FROM MY AGENT, David Egdes. He wanted to draft a press release about my illness. I fought him on it, asking, "Who's going to care?" He ignored my resistance and faxed it to me at the hospital the next day. I approved it, but I still didn't understand why he was being so insistent. It wasn't going to be big news or anything. Yes, I was sick, but people get sick every day. We didn't need to announce it to the whole world.

Before I knew it, CNN, ESPN, and a score of other media outlets were reporting the story; there were also articles in *USA Today* and the *New York Post*. I didn't care about any of that—what I *did* care about was the flood of support I received. It was unlike anything I could have ever imagined.

The night of that press release, my mom came home to 27 messages on her answering machine. I was inundated with letters from people around the world, many of whom I'd never even met. My room filled up with flowers, balloons, and food. Friends would call every day, send gifts, and come to visit. Two pals of mine on the Tour, Lisa Raymond and Rennae Stubbs, actually sent me a present every day. One day it was a blanket; the next day, cookies; the next, an assortment of bandanas for the inevitable hair loss . . . you name it, they thought of it. The whole thing was surreal, and so incredibly uplifting that I still find it difficult to describe. Lying in that hospital bed, fighting for my life, it meant the world to me that all these people were rallying behind me. They wanted me to stick around, and that gave me a tremendous amount of strength.

With my family camped out in my room most of the time, I had very little time to feel sorry for myself. We found the humor in everything, and we laughed—a lot. One day about a week into my stay, my mom pulled up my pajama pants for my daily massage, and I was stunned by how atrophied my calves had become. "Where did my calves go?" I jokingly asked her.

"I don't know," she replied. Then she added, "But your hips are still there!"

We just started cracking up. I loved that despite the circumstances, my sweet, sensitive mother had made a joke at my expense.

A few days later, on a night when Andrew had gone home to rest, my brother was sleeping in the chair next to me, and our father was laid out on the air mattress on the floor. Dad started snoring, loudly, and woke the two of us up. I mean, he was sawing some serious logs. Mircea and I were just lying there wide-awake, giggling. The walls would reverberate with the echo, then Dad would quiet down for a moment, then start up again. My brother started saying, "Crrressss-scendo, *de*crrrrressscendo," in concert with the symphonic melodies our father was producing. Giddy from the lack of sleep, we laughed so hard we were literally crying. But that was the kind of laughter that kept the sad tears away.

As it turned out, my brother wasn't just there to make me laugh. About a week into my stay, he probably saved my life. The night in question, I was in bed, strapped to my IV pole. Mircea was trying to sleep in the makeshift La-Z-Boy next to me when I started coughing. It worsened to the point where I couldn't take a breath. This went on too long for my brother's comfort, so he called the nurse to come take my vital signs, and asked that she call the intern.

The intern came in, listened to my lungs, and declared that I simply needed some Robitussin. I couldn't inhale without coughing, and this guy wanted to give me cough syrup! Mircea wasn't buying it. He told the intern to contact the attending physician, and to do a "pulse ox."

A pulse-oximeter test is a simple procedure. A gauge placed on your finger measures the amount of oxygen in your bloodstream as a percentage. A normal reading is between 98 and 100 percent. Eighty is bad; I was at sixty. In other words, grossly, dangerously abnormal. The intern thought the machine was faulty, so my brother suggested that they try another one. The second pulse-ox-machine reading was even worse, in the low 50s. My *body* was malfunctioning, not the machine.

Within minutes, there were six people in my room, and an x-ray machine was being pushed through the door to examine my lungs. They immediately gave me an oxygen mask hooked up to a tank on the wall. It wasn't until I inhaled that pure flow of sweet unobstructed oxygen at four liters per minute that I realized how bad things really were. I felt like I'd been breathing through mud.

It turned out that I had developed pulmonary edema, basically fluid filling my lungs, which Mircea knew was a possible complication of my oral chemotherapy. If my brother hadn't been there, I would have taken the Robitussin without complaint, and my lungs could have completely filled with fluid by morning. I could have ended up with a breathing tube down my throat . . . or worse, I could have died.

Treatment for the edema had me on oxygen for a week while I started a regime of steroids to flush the fluid from my lungs. Because I was hooked up to the oxygen tank on the wall, I couldn't leave my bed. I was forced to use a bedside commode and get sponge baths. Any shred of dignity I might have been clinging to was officially thrown out the window.

After the fluid cleared, I slowly restarted the oral chemo, but the steroids blessed me with a whole new look: a very swollen "moon face," as it is so affectionately called. About that time, my friend Kim Po came to visit. She'd been in Strasbourg, France, playing a lead-up tournament to the French Open. She had a two-day window in her schedule, so she flew across the Atlantic with her husband, Oliver, to see me for the weekend, before flying back to France for the second Grand Slam of the year. It was one of the most impressive displays of support and friendship I have ever received. I knew Kim was expecting my face to be gaunt, so when she walked into my room, I could see the shock in her eyes. I tried to bring some levity to the situation by saying, "Not the look you were expecting, huh?"

Getting back to my brother, while he and I had spent a lot of time together over the years, some of our fondest memories have come from that month in the hospital. Although he spent hours every day reading me the voluminous stacks of mail that came in, it was his dark, sarcastic sense of humor—"Hey, check out Corina's gigantic bruise!"— that kept me semi-sane. He also rented inspirational movies like *The Shawshank Redemption,* which features the classic line about how you either get busy living or get busy dying. It became my mantra.

WHILE I WAS IN THE HOSPITAL, I watched quite a bit of tennis on TV, the highlight being the 2001 French Open, which started about ten days into my stay. As I watched religiously every day, I began to see the sport in a whole new light. I always regarded tennis as great entertainment, but I never really thought it helped others in any tangible way. I used to laugh when people made a big deal about the fact that I was a tennis player while my brother and parents were the ones dedicated to saving lives. I was good at hitting a little yellow ball over a net; *they* were good at keeping people alive. Few would ever exclaim to my mom, "Oh my God, your son is a doctor? Amazing!" But someone would invariably gasp, "Oh my God, your daughter is a professional tennis player? She's been to Wimbledon? She *won* Wimbledon? Wow!"

My attitude shifted while I sat in that hospital bed watching the French Open. I still don't compare playing a sport to saving lives, but I did start to see the value of my profession from an entirely different perspective.

About halfway through the tournament, I had a minor surgical procedure to install a port in my chest to provide a more permanent form of IV access. I was running out of veins at that point, and since I had about seven more months of chemo and blood draws ahead of me, it was a necessary evil. Unfortunately, the muscles in my chest were well developed from years of swinging a tennis racket, making the procedure more traumatic than anticipated.

That was just the beginning of the trauma associated with my new little device. I was watching the French Open with friends and family on the day the nurse decided to "access" the port. In other words, she had to stick needles into the port's two chambers so she could inject me with drugs. Everyone cleared from the room, and the nurse came in and covered my chest with iodine and sterile napkins. She then injected a needle into my chest, which was already sore as hell from the implantation of the port, at a 90-degree angle. Unfortunately for me, this woman had no clue what she was doing. Repeatedly she missed the chamber, sticking the needles in over and over. She was absolutely torturing me.

Meanwhile, on TV there was a fourth-round match between Gustavo "Guga" Kuerten, two-time French Open Champion, and American Michael Russell. Michael, whom I barely knew, was clearly the underdog, but he was battling and winning, unfazed by the occasion. I loved watching Guga, one of the most graceful, not to mention humble, players on the Tour, but I found myself cheering for the underdog, captivated by his fighting spirit. As the drama unfolded, I was engrossed in the match, celebrating every winner and agonizing over every error. Michael held match point, but Guga came back to win the match and eventually, his third French Open. But as far as I was concerned, Michael won something just as important that day.

As I watched this enthralling match, I forgot about the nurse torturing me with the needle. The tennis was the only thing that kept me from going berserk. At that moment I remember thinking, *Maybe playing tennis for a living is _not_ that insignificant.* Here I was, in virtual agony, captivated by these two guys playing their hearts out on the court. Their spirit and conviction was contagious. Watching them was more than an amusing distraction; it was an inspiration.

From the outside looking in, I realized the profound impact sports can have on people. Supporting a team or an athlete gives us a chance to feel like we're part of something bigger than ourselves. At times, it gives us the opportunity to escape our personal reality. Ignited by passion and united by common desire, we cheer, we dream—and we hope.

During the French Open, Lindsay flew into town with her husband-to-be, Jonathan Leach. She'd recently suffered a severe bone bruise in her knee, an injury that forced her to withdraw from the tournament. Once again, I was touched that my friends were making such an effort to visit me.

Unfortunately, the weekend they arrived I was experiencing another prolonged nosebleed episode. That Sunday morning, the bleeding was going full force; after two hours of ice, gauze, and every other therapy available, I decided to get up and take a shower. Showering was the highlight of my day. It was my one chance to get disconnected from the IV, and it was one of the few things that made me feel human. My father was the only one there on this particular day, and he was hovering as usual. He was apprehensive about my taking a shower in my condition, but I assured him that I was fine. I got unhooked from the IV, closed the bathroom door, and started running the water. As soon as I stepped into the shower, my foot slipped. And I fell right on the floor. Hard. As soon as I made impact, my nose started spewing blood.

Instantly, my dad was at the door, wanting to come in and help. I was in intense pain, but I didn't want to worry him, so I held him off while I finished a quick shower. I realized I couldn't dry off while also tending to the blood pouring from my nose, so I finally enlisted his help. He came in to the sight of his bloody, stark-naked daughter and helped me dry off. We took turns: I held the tissue while he dried, then he held the tissue while *I* dried. It was simultaneously comic and frightening. It was scary because the bleeding could have escalated into something much more serious, but the awkwardness of the situation made it almost funny. Dad was extremely upset that I had fallen on "his watch," so from that point on, I wasn't allowed to shower unsupervised. I felt a little like I was in a women's detention facility—I had to be monitored at all times.

When Lindsay showed up that Sunday, I was still a mess. I could tell it was hard on her. I remember her boyfriend, Jon, clutching her hand as she attempted to stay strong for me. I tried to be strong for her as well. The nurse had just given me IV Benadryl, and I became incredibly sleepy and totally loopy. I used every ounce of my energy to stay coherent and not fall asleep. I was so grateful that my friend had come to see me, and I wanted to show my appreciation by staying awake and talking to her. It didn't occur to me that I was mumbling in incomplete sentences and she couldn't understand a damn word I was saying anyway.

THROUGHOUT MY STAY AT JACKSON MEMORIAL, I rarely got emotional. I cried a few times before I got in, and definitely shed many tears after I got out, but I stayed pretty even-tempered while there, with two notable exceptions. The first was the day I was allowed outside. I'd been cooped up in my hospital room for three weeks at that point, and I was begging to make one, just one, brief trip outside. My daily question was: "Can I go out today?" The day the doctor determined I was stable enough, I was ecstatic!

I had to wear a mask and get unhooked from all the IVs, but with Andrew and Mircea holding me on both sides, I went outside for ten minutes. With tears streaming down my cheeks, I sat down, let the sun shine on my face, and listened to the birds singing—things I had always taken for granted. I felt two distinct, and very different, emotions: sadness and gratitude. I was grateful for the opportunity, but at the same time, reality came crashing down on me. This is what my life had become. My time in the hospital seemed so surreal that I could almost convince myself it was all a dream. It was in the moments that gave me a glimpse of "real" life—my old life—that I realized how dramatically my world had changed.

The other tearful moment occurred during the French Open. I'd been in touch with a lot of the players who were competing there— old friends like Lisa and Rennae would call almost daily to see how I was doing. One night, Rennae called and told Andrew to make sure I watched Jennifer Capriati play her quarterfinal match the next day against Serena Williams. I *had* to watch? Something was up.

I'd been keeping up with the tournament from the beginning, but because of the time difference, Jennifer and Serena's match was being broadcast in the morning, and I happened to be sound asleep. Mircea and company didn't have the heart to wake me up, so they taped the match, and I viewed it that afternoon.

I watched Jennifer and Serena meet with the chair umpire at the net for the coin toss, as is customary in tennis. But I never could have expected what came next. With the camera focused right on her, Jennifer held up a big sign that said: GET WELL SOON, CORINA. The crowd broke into applause, and I broke into tears. It was such a wonderful surprise. Once again, I was overwhelmed.

I later found out that all of the players had gotten together, wanting to do something special for me, and Jennifer had volunteered to hold up the sign on behalf of everyone on the Tour. I didn't know Jennifer that well at the time, but I was touched that she had offered to make the gesture public. It was accompanied by a more private gesture: a poster signed by every one of the players, which the Tour staff had framed and sent to me in the hospital. I knew firsthand that the tennis world was competitive, cutthroat, and, at times, divisive. Such is the nature of individual sports. But what I didn't know is that in the face of tragedy, the tennis world could unite to this extent in support of one of its own.

TOWARD THE END OF MY STAY OF CLOSE TO A MONTH, the chemo started taking its full effect, and my hair began to fall out. I wanted my brother to shave my head, but it took a couple days of my hair coming out in massive clumps before I mustered up the courage. I finally looked at him and said, "Okay, it's time . . . it's looking pretty straggly." Mircea looked at me with his trademark wry grin and replied, "It's looked like that for a while now."

I put on a hospital gown, sat up in a chair, and told my brother to go to town. He took the clippers out and began shaving, but in the middle of the process, I could tell he was up to something. I saw the smirk on his face—he was enjoying himself way too much. He finally announced, "You're done!" My immediate response was, "What did you do?" I looked in the mirror to see what Mircea considered an artistic hairdo. He had shaved the entire back and sides of my head, leaving a two-inch spike in the front. It was hysterical. I looked like a badass biker chick.

When we finally stopped laughing, Mircea took a series of mug shots, front and profile, and then shaved off the rest of my hair. We both put bandanas on and took another round of pictures. I was completely bald, but I didn't care. If losing my hair meant that I was going to live, then so be it. My brother and I made the best of it. In this situation, like so many times during this ordeal, I had two choices: I could laugh or cry. More often than not, I chose to laugh.

The last week in the hospital was spent anxiously waiting to get out. The chemotherapy had destroyed the few blood cells I had left, so I had to wait for my body to build up a new reserve of these vital cells in my bone marrow. My white-blood-cell count was especially critical because without that integral part of my immune system, any infection could become life threatening. The counts had to reach a certain level before I could be released, so every day my family and I would wait for my blood counts, hoping that my cells were regenerating quickly. And every day, we were disappointed. It took forever for my counts to increase. My bone marrow apparently did *not* have my work ethic—it was incredibly lazy. To make matters worse, I developed a fever. One of my IV sites became infected, so my stay was extended yet again. I was miserable and frustrated. I just wanted to go home.

Finally, the fever went down, my counts reached the desired level, and I was discharged. I was free! Mircea drove me home in his convertible, so I could feel the sun on my face for a full hour. We both had tears of joy streaming down our faces as we drove away from Jackson Memorial Hospital, which had been both my salvation and my prison for the past month. But we were also both smiling, and the wind on the highway eventually dried our tears. I was ecstatic to get home and indulge in the small pleasures (like going to the bathroom without an IV pole) that I'd always taken for granted.

After I settled in at home, I went back to Jackson Memorial for another bone-marrow test, my first since I'd gone into treatment weeks earlier. It came back negative—I was in remission. I wasn't completely out of the woods, and there were more rounds of chemo to come, but at that moment, the cancer was gone.

WE HAD A CELEBRATORY DINNER AT MY PARENTS' HOUSE: my mother and father, my brother and sister-in-law, and my husband and me. At one point my dad said, "Corina, there's an Adidas box for you in the garage." Cancer or not, I still had an endorsement deal with Adidas, so I went to check out the latest shipment.

There was no box in the garage. Instead, much to my surprise, there was a brand-new BMW SUV sitting there. During my stay in the hospital, for reasons I can't explain, I became obsessed with getting this particular vehicle. I was just joking, of course—I wasn't sure I'd ever be driving again, so I certainly didn't need a new car. But my generous, thoughtful father had taken my jokes and made them a reality. For me, the BMW was so much more than a car; it was a symbol of hope, survival, and family.

I had a couple weeks to relax at home before I had to start my second round of chemo. The doctor told me from the beginning that I'd have to go through three separate courses of chemo to ensure that my cancer stayed in remission. For the time being, I could forget about treatment or anything else to do with my future. I spent my time at home, enjoying and appreciating every moment. I pored over the hundreds of letters and cards I'd received, and I responded to each and every one. I was so touched that people had gone out of their way to write that I figured it was the least I could do.

The third Grand Slam of the year, Wimbledon, started while I was home recuperating. I watched from my couch as my friends played. By that point, I felt good enough to do a few media interviews, and Wimbledon seemed like the perfect occasion. I did two live television interviews via satellite from my home in Florida. I was back, albeit distantly, at the place where I'd celebrated one of my greatest achievements: winning the 1999 women's doubles championship with my dear friend and partner, Lindsay, who was now back playing at the All England Club. She wore a necklace with the letter C on it throughout the entire tournament. Even though I wasn't on the court playing with her that year, I felt like I was there in spirit.

As a professional player, the four "Slams" are the touchstones of one's career. In this case, the 2001 Wimbledon tournament was a touchstone of *my* life. I didn't know if I would ever play tennis again—in fact, at the time, I assumed I wouldn't. But I did know that I was fighting through one of the darkest chapters of my life. Winning Wimbledon was great. But just watching Wimbledon in my new condition was even greater.

• • •   • • •

Chapter 4

NEW REALITY

As I sat there watching the 2001 Wimbledon unfold on television, I couldn't help but be swept back to two years before and note the huge chasm between my life then and my life now. I tried to forget my health crisis, just for a minute, and take myself fully back to that time when I felt I'd accomplished something truly special.

WINNING THE WIMBLEDON DOUBLES TITLE IN '99 was a dream come true. As a player, the focus is on performing well at the Grand Slams, and one schedules training and other tournaments in order to peak at those four major tournaments. I would have been thrilled to win *any* Grand Slam, but winning at Wimbledon—the oldest tennis tournament in history and the Slam that many consider to be the most prestigious— was especially gratifying.

What made it all the more special is that I shared the victory with Lindsay, who just happened to be one of the best players in women's tennis. Lindsay also won the singles title at Wimbledon that year, after having won the U.S. Open the year before. (She would then go on to win the Australian Open the year after.) We became doubles partners when she was at the height of her brilliant singles career, so the timing was perfect for me.

Becoming a doubles team was actually Lindsay's idea. Right before the French Open in '99, Lindsay e-mailed me to ask if I wanted to team up with her to play that tournament and Wimbledon. I was ranked in the 20s as a singles player at the time, and most of my energy was focused there. But I'd been very successful in doubles as a junior, and I was starting to have some success in the pros. I'd already won two doubles titles that year, one with my good friend Kim Po in Tokyo, and one with Larisa Neiland in the Gold Coast in Australia.

I'd always loved playing doubles, which I think is one of the reasons why I excelled at it. I loved the team aspect of the game: I enjoyed having someone out there with me, someone to talk to and strategize with, someone to help weather the ups and downs of a match. I also had a good instinct for doubles, since I had played it growing up and understood the intricacies of the game. Doubles involves more volleying, or returning the ball before it bounces, and this was a skill my father had championed from the beginning. Whenever I played doubles as a kid, Dad made me serve and volley, and I became comfortable with the rhythm of it. I was also naturally quick with my hands, and my reflexes served me well in the fast-paced exchanges that often occur in doubles. My feet, unfortunately, were another story. Foot speed was never my forte, and I always joke that my talent was distributed to the upper half of my body. My movement wasn't as much of a liability in doubles because I only had to cover half the court, so it masked my weaknesses and played into my strengths.

As for Lindsay's offer, I *was* available for Wimbledon, but unfortunately I'd already committed to someone else for the French. Tennis can be ruthless at times, as I've noted, and some players might have broken a prior commitment to play with someone of Lindsay's caliber. I can't lie—I seriously thought about breaking my previous commitment, but ultimately, I just couldn't bring myself to do it. I went ahead and played the French with another partner, and we lost in the early rounds.

Wimbledon was only the second time I'd played with Lindsay, and really the first extended time. Right away I noticed a distinct difference in our approach to the game. Lindsay was confident; she was already a Grand Slam singles champion. I, on the other hand, had never made it past the third round of a Grand Slam in *any* event. This was a huge opportunity for me, and I was terrified that I'd screw it up. We'd take the court for a match, and once we'd established a lead, she'd be talking about the next match. I was feeling nervous about the current match, and she'd already be on to the next one.

I also felt a tremendous amount of pressure to keep up. Lindsay played extremely well those two weeks—so well, in fact, that I joked that she could have won the doubles that year with my grandmother. She stormed through the singles and ended up winning the most prestigious title in tennis without losing a set. We didn't lose a single set on our way to the doubles title, either, which was due to Lindsay, and also because the draw favored us at every turn. The highly seeded veteran doubles teams kept losing before we had to play them. They were upset in the early rounds, and we ended up playing teams we were favored to beat going in. It was a huge opportunity, and I was very uptight before every match, hoping I wouldn't blow it.

I HAD MY SHARE OF STRESS OFF THE COURT AS WELL. Grand Slams are physically and mentally exhausting. The pressure is heightened, and demands on a player's time increase. Plus, the waiting around that characterizes most tennis tournaments is even more pronounced at Wimbledon due to the frequent rain delays.

The days are long; the site is packed with fans, players, coaches, and organizers; and everyone expends a lot of energy just running into people they know. As a result, players put a premium on keeping their time away from the courts as stress free and low-key as possible. This was all the more critical for me because I'd already been on the road for ten weeks, playing lead-up tournaments to the French and Wimbledon. I was already worn-out heading into that fortnight in England, all the more reason to conserve my energy off the court and focus solely on my tennis. But things didn't quite work out that way.

My brother used his vacation time to come to Wimbledon with his then girlfriend, Laura. He'd traveled with me many times before, and it wasn't unusual for him to come see me play in his free time. He understood the pressures of tournament play, and I always loved having him around.

I rented a two-bedroom flat in Wimbledon Village for the length of the tournament so we could all stay together. One of the unique things about Wimbledon is that most players elect to rent a house or an apartment in the village, which is about a ten-minute walk from the All England Club. This is a welcome change from the anonymous hotel rooms players stay in week after week. The village is small and quaint, with great restaurants within walking distance. After a long day on the courts, it's really nice to grab a bite to eat or get takeout—my usual preference—nearby. (I guess you could cook as well, although I don't know of any players who actually use their kitchen for that purpose!)

I so looked forward to settling in and creating a home away from home. Off the court, I wanted to do nothing more than order in, watch TV, and hide in my apartment. Laura, however, had different ideas. She'd taken her two weeks of vacation to come to London and understandably didn't expect to be cooped up in a flat 45 minutes from downtown, catering to *my* schedule.

My brother and I didn't see each other that often in those days, so we wanted to spend as much time together as possible and didn't want to split up for dinners. The first week was spent just the way I like it: in the village, relaxing and eating locally. I made the third round of singles but eventually lost to Steffi Graf at the end of that week. By that time, Laura and Mircea were getting a little stir-crazy, wanting to go into London at night for dinner. I felt obliged to join them because they'd accommodated me the first week. I also wanted to spend time with my brother.

Unfortunately, the second week was plagued by rain delays. Lindsay and I would be on the schedule for the day, but then we'd end up sitting in the players' lounge or the locker room watching the rain come down. By the end of the day, I was totally drained. It was mentally taxing to wait at the courts for hours, hoping to play, while trying to stay focused and mentally prepared. All I wanted to do was go back to the apartment and veg in front of the TV—but instead, I would clean up and then spend 45 minutes on the tube with Andrew to join Mircea and Laura in London. The stress of everything was slowly driving me nuts, and I made no effort to hide my irritation when I showed up for dinner.

Finally, the last evening Mircea and Laura were in town, and the night before my quarterfinal doubles match, I showed up for dinner in a typically pissed-off mood. My brother made a snide remark about my less-than-sunny disposition, and I just lost it. We ended up in a screaming match, a rarity for us, in the middle of some bar in down-town London. This escalated into another screaming match, this time between Laura and my brother, outside the restaurant after dinner.

The argument continued at a fever pitch back at the apartment. Since the walls were paper-thin, I could hear most of it, and I barely slept. I felt awful about arguing with my brother, and I was saddened that in an effort to please both Laura and me, he'd ended up getting yelled at from both sides. By the time I woke up, they were on their way back to America, as previously planned, leaving me a note of apology.

When I got to the courts to warm up for the match, I was a mess. I couldn't keep a ball in the court. I tried to appear calm on the outside, but internally, I was completely freaking out. I kept thinking that I was going to blow the biggest opportunity of my career and completely embarrass myself in the quarterfinals of Wimbledon. Luckily, before Lindsay and I were about to play, the clouds opened and the rain poured. Our match was canceled and rescheduled for the next day.

I practically skipped back to the apartment knowing I had escaped potential disaster. I was equally ecstatic that I didn't have a 45-minute trek to London ahead of me. I recovered from the drama of the week and got back to focusing on winning Wimbledon.

Because of all the rain that week, things got terribly backed up. All of the finals—men's and women's, singles and doubles—were scheduled for that last Sunday. Lindsay had to play the doubles final within hours of playing the singles final. She beat Steffi Graf, 6-4, 7-5, to claim her second Grand Slam title, her first at Wimbledon. We had a brief champagne celebration in the locker room (neither of us actually drank champagne) and took the court shortly thereafter in the doubles final against Mariaan de Swardt and Elena Tatarkova. This was it for me. My first Grand Slam final . . . the finals of Wimbledon.

I walked on the court with butterflies in my stomach, but once the match began, I found a rhythm and managed to put the enormity of the occasion aside. I tried to play one point at a time and focus on handling things on my side of the court. Lindsay was playing well, and I felt we could win the match comfortably as long as I didn't screw things up. I also knew that this was the first Grand Slam final for our opponents, so I was grateful to have the only player with any experience in this situation on my side of the net.

Lindsay and I had a 6-4, 5-4 lead after breaking serve midway through the second set. We went to sit down for the 90-second changeover before what we hoped would be the last game of the match. Lindsay was going to serve the next game, thank God, because buoyed by confidence or not, I was beginning to get so nervous that I wasn't sure I could hold on to my racket. I got up to walk the 20 feet to my position on the court and became so dizzy that I swear the earth started moving beneath me. The court felt like a seesaw. I'd been anxious before and during matches, but I had never experienced anything like that.

I tried to steady myself, but before I knew it, we were down 15-40 and on the verge of losing the game. We managed to pull even, and Lindsay served at deuce. Mariaan hit a return up the middle that was my ball to hit, but I was so nervous that I think I actually moved to avoid hitting it. Lindsay lunged, and in a remarkable effort, not only got her racket on it, but hit a deep reply. Mariaan hit a lob, and although I struggled to move my feet, I somehow got back to put the overhead away.

Match point. Lindsay hit a great serve and teed off on Elena's short return. Elena managed to get her racket on the ball, and I found myself moving forward for a sitter forehand volley to win Wimbledon—and all I could think was: *Please don't miss it!* I put the ball away. Lindsay and I screamed in celebration and jumped into each other's arms. I was ecstatic, but I remember being impressed that Lindsay was equally excited. She'd won the singles title at Wimbledon and seemed just as happy to win the doubles. It made the experience even more gratifying to know that she cared so much.

As we waited for the trophy ceremony, I sat on Lindsay's lap, put my arm around her, and thanked her. I told her that this was something I never thought I would accomplish, and I would never forget that she contacted me in the first place. She believed in me enough to ask me to play with her, and I knew that I owed this victory to her.

After the trophy presentation and attendant hoopla, I escaped to the players' restaurant. I sat in a booth in the empty eatery and collapsed with relief. I was so thankful that the whole thing was over. The stress of trying to perform, trying to keep up, and trying to make my family happy was finally gone. I was incredibly grateful for the experience, but mostly what I felt at that moment was relief. Massive, liberating relief.

The rest of the day was spent getting ready for the Champions' Ball, another one of the unique traditions at Wimbledon. The All England Club holds a black-tie extravaganza on the last Sunday of the tournament in honor of all the champions of that year—and since tennis players don't usually travel with black-tie attire, the tournament provides the appropriate garb for the champions and their guests. I went down to the locker room and was greeted by a rack of formal gowns to choose from. I picked out my dress, and Andrew got a tux; we were then left with about an hour to head back to the apartment, shower, and leave for the ball.

Still riding the high of the day, Lindsay and I went to the event with her coach at the time, Robert Van't Hof, and Andrew. As prestigious as it is, this affair can be a little stuffy, so we were all jazzed up by the idea of partying in London afterward to really let loose and celebrate. Unfortunately, the ball lasted much longer than we had anticipated, and by the time everything was said and done, we were exhausted. Gone were our grand plans for the evening. We all had morning flights, so we called it a night.

Andrew and I flew home and immediately took off again for a four-day vacation in the Bahamas with our good friends Kristine and Damien Kunce. More than anything, I used those four days to decompress from the stress of the previous two weeks. We definitely celebrated, but the focus was more on relaxing and spending quality time with each other. After a week, I was right back to practicing twice a day and preparing for the summer tournaments in the States that lead up to the U.S. Open.

My life didn't change much after winning Wimbledon, and I think about that to this day because it gives me a great perspective. I had a Wimbledon title and deposited a substantial check in the bank, which was extremely gratifying, but the focus shifted quickly. I started think-ing about the next week, the next tournament, and then the next year, when Lindsay and I would have to defend our title. The challenge went from *getting* to the top to *staying* there.

I always thought that if I could accomplish something extra-ordinary like winning Wimbledon, my life would be so much better. I could play tennis freely because of what I'd achieved. I wouldn't care about results as much anymore because, hey, I'd won Wimbledon! I had this vision of what it would feel like—the endless joy that win-ning a Grand Slam would bring me—yet I found myself in that empty restaurant, just happy that the whole thing was over. Not exactly the emotion I was expecting.

Looking back on winning Wimbledon, I realize this: goals and dreams are important, but true joy comes from enjoying the process and appre-ciating what you have in the moment. Of course that's easier said than done, but by solely focusing on the ultimate goal, you're forever chasing your tail, looking to fill a never-ending abyss of ifs. *If I could just win one more tournament, if I could just win a Grand Slam, if I could just make a mil-lion dollars (or two or ten), then I will be happy. . . .* It never ends.

When I look back now, I'm so proud of what I accomplished. I still think it's cool to go to the All England Club and see my name on the champions' wall, but as I've come to learn over the past few years, my career achievements don't define me, and they never did.

I CAME BACK TO THE REALITY I WAS FACING TWO YEARS after my Wimble-don victory. I was dealing with the fact that I was going to have to go through more chemo. You see, when I initially arrived at Jackson Memorial for that first long month of treatment, Dr. Goodman told me that no matter what the state of the cancer was when I left the hospital, I was going to have to endure a total of three courses of che-motherapy. This was the minimum requirement to ensure that I had a chance of long-term survival. I only had a few weeks to go home, relax, and give my body a chance to recover slightly before I started the second round of chemo.

Leaving the hospital was a bittersweet experience. I thoroughly enjoyed my time at home, appreciating the things I'd once taken for granted. I answered letters and happily watched Wimbledon from my couch, but I slowly fell into a state of emotional limbo. I felt caught between the high-drama world of the hospital and "real life," and what that meant for me. Being diagnosed with leukemia and then being hospitalized for a month was an all-consuming event. There was a constant bustle of activity and attention—on top of one medical procedure after another, there were all of the cards and letters, visits from family and friends, greetings from the French Open, and so on. I was caught up in every moment. It was like being in a battle zone or some other type of high drama. My focus was laser sharp: get well, do what they ask, don't die.

I didn't feel particularly depressed or anxious the first month in the hospital, since there were too many distractions. At home, however, the distractions were largely gone, and I was left to emotionally fend for myself. My new reality as a cancer patient became painfully obvious. I was in my old house with a completely new life. Sadness, loneliness, and confusion began to replace gratitude, appreciation, and joy.

By the time I started my second round of chemo, everyone in my family was back at work, so I'd drive myself down to the hospital to get the treatment on an outpatient basis. The IV chemo always made me incredibly nauseated and completely destroyed my appetite. All I could stomach were smoothies from Jamba Juice, and there was one right off the highway on my way back home to Boca. I'd religiously stop, pick up a smoothie, and then go home and get back in bed. That was my meal, and my excursion, for the day.

Except for the necessary trips to Miami for treatment, I was generally too sick and exhausted to get out of bed. When the second round of chemo started taking effect, I developed a new set of physical problems as well, the worst being strange and excruciating rectal pain that only intensified with time. At first I didn't mention this to anyone; I was embarrassed and had no idea what the hell was going on. I suffered in silence for days until I came down with a fever. This was a red flag, because an infection can be deadly when your immune system has been obliterated by chemical poison. I immediately called the doctor, who asked if there were any other problems besides the fever. I reluctantly explained the searing pain in my rear end. He replied, "Oh, that can be a side effect of the chemo." Now they tell me!

By the time Andrew drove me to the hospital in Miami, my fever was a raging 104. I was also shaking, almost convulsing, uncontrollably. Nurses smothered me in blankets to mitigate the shaking, but the fever remained. In fact, it remained for the next four days. The doctors couldn't find the source of the infection, making it impossible to treat. They tried one antibiotic after another. Nothing worked.

Meanwhile, a whole new me emerged from this ordeal: a raving bitch. The fever was torturous, but it paled in comparison to the posterior pain—which was sharp, unrelenting, and completely put me over the edge. The extreme discomfort had finally overpowered my ability to put on a brave face. I became short-tempered and irritable, snapping at any poor soul who came near me.

To top things off, Jackson Memorial is a teaching hospital. The good news about teaching hospitals is that they're on the cutting edge of new treatments. The bad news is that they also use their patients as real-life teaching lessons. When you least expect it, a group of earnest medical students suddenly fills your room as an attending doctor explains your case. You're not a *person* to these people; you're a disease with a person attached. You're all platelet formations and blood counts (and, in my case, severe rectal pain). "So, students, what do we think of Corina's chronic rectal pain? Let's take a look!" The situation was beyond embarrassing.

The doctor finally told me that he was going to try a different antibiotic for the fever, called amphotericin b. That sounded fine to me until he added that, around the hospital, they called it "amphoterrible" or "shake and bake"—which didn't seem very encouraging. It turns out that "shake and bake" is an apt catchphrase, as the side effects of this particular drug include fever, chills, nausea, and vomiting. It sounded like I was potentially trading one type of agony for another, but, hey, I was willing to try anything that might help.

I was given a test dose and felt no ill effects. About ten minutes later, as I stepped out of my daily shower, I began violently shaking from the chills and baking from a new fever. The nurse administered IV Benadryl to stop the shaking. It worked. She then offered me IV Demerol in concert with the Benadryl. I momentarily considered refusing it, as I'd tried to avoid painkillers throughout my stay in the hospital, but then I thought, *Why not? I might as well try it.* I received the

Demerol straight into my bloodstream through the port in my chest, and my many discomforts vanished in a heartbeat. The pain instantly ceased. I was euphoric (in more ways than one!). I immediately said to the nurse, "I'm going to be getting more of that!" Which I did—every four hours, every time I was in the hospital, because that damn rectal pain stayed with me in varying degrees for the next nine months of my life.

The second round of chemo knocked me on my ass—pardon the pun—and I wasn't looking forward to the third. To make matters worse, on the day I was being discharged, Dr. Goodman entered my room and announced that I'd have to undergo a *fourth* round. He told me that because my platelet count had been so low when I was first diagnosed, a fourth treatment would be necessary to ensure that my cancer stayed in remission.

I was absolutely devastated by this news. I cried in the hospital, then went home and cried some more. I told my mom about the added round, and she later told me that "tears were springing" from my eyes. I was sure that it would take every sinew of mental toughness just to endure one more of those hideous treatments, and now I was facing two. As I said, the novelty of the whole experience was long gone, as was my ever-present cheering squad. No more stuffed animals, balloons, or bouquets arrived daily. Back at Jackson, my treatments now took place in the bone-marrow unit, and my hospital room really looked like a hospital room—not a suite at the Plaza. This was my new reality.

PERHAPS THE BIGGEST CHANGE IN MY DAILY LIFE WAS my husband's absence. Because Andrew was my tennis coach, and I was out of commission, he needed to find other work. An opening quickly arose at a country club about 40 minutes north of our home in Boca, and Andrew took it. This was a huge shift. Andrew Turcinovich had been my constant companion since I was 15, first as my coach, then as my coach/boyfriend, and finally as my coach/husband.

I initially met Andrew through another coach of mine, Joe Brooke. Joe and Andrew had worked together in Singapore, and when Joe returned to Florida, Andrew came with him. Andrew was a terrific coach. He was astute about the technicalities of the game, and he rarely raised his voice, which was a welcome change from my dad. At the time, Joe and Andrew worked with a group of guys and one 14-year-old girl (me), and we'd practice together every day after school. Around the same time, my dad decided that I should travel to more tournaments to build up my Junior credentials, and no one in my family could make that kind of time commitment. Andrew didn't have a family tying him down, and he impressed my dad as both proficient at tennis and trustworthy as a person, so he got the job.

Andrew developed feelings for me when I was 15 and he was 26, but I saw him as my coach and traveling companion, nothing else. We were traveling in Europe at one point soon after he signed on, and he made an awkward attempt to kiss me. I reacted by screeching, "What are you doing?!" I was shocked and unnerved by the situation. I was just a teenager, and had no idea how to handle it.

Andrew was forward from the start, but this is not an uncommon occurrence on the women's Tour. There are many coaches who are both predatory and controlling, and they find ways to solidify that control. Female players mature faster than their male counterparts, at least physically, and are regularly in the advanced ranks at 14, 15, and 16. Many travel with either an overbearing parent—who often has a blatant economic interest—or a coach. The players are young, vulnerable, and isolated; and they're in a very high-pressure, competitive environment. They long for a connection with someone. In my case, I don't think Andrew was looking to control every aspect of my life, but his advances were clearly inappropriate. He was an older man whom I both looked up to and sought direction from, not to mention traveled the world with.

Although Andrew had crossed the line, over time I found a way to make it all okay. The situation went from disturbing to exciting to comfortable. I didn't tell anyone what was evolving, but I somehow rationalized that it was all appropriate and made sense for my life. By the time my parents learned about the relationship, Andrew was so firmly cemented in the family that no one questioned the wisdom or appropriateness of the affair. As long as I was "happy" and my tennis wasn't negatively affected, it was all okay.

My parents loved Andrew and came to think of him as their third child. As my dad says, "He was very laid-back and low-key, and I had 100 percent trust in him. He was not just polite; he was respectful."

In defense of my parents, they never suspected anything untoward was going on because I never said a word about it until I turned 17. I kept it a secret from the entire world. As things evolved, I grew into the relationship and accepted it as natural, if not inevitable. At 19, I started to doubt the entire arrangement, but I didn't have the strength or life experience to do anything about it. I was well into my professional career and couldn't imagine breaking up with Andrew—my coach, my close friend, my boyfriend, and my one-man support network. He filled so many roles in my life that I couldn't distinguish one from the other. I'd never traveled by myself or pursued tennis on my own, so the thought of cutting Andrew out of my life was simply too daunting.

Perhaps the biggest decision I made to ensure that this man would remain a part of my life was my decision not to attend college. My family placed education at the very top of life's priorities, but my father never demanded that I go to college and pursue a certain profession, as *his* father had done. He must have thought it unnecessary.

In my senior year of high school, I was offered a full tennis scholarship to the University of California, Los Angeles (UCLA), and I initially accepted. We all assumed that I'd spend at least a year in college before turning pro. That was certainly Mircea's advice. And had I gone to UCLA, it's likely that Andrew and I would have drifted apart. I probably would have found a whole new set of interests and an entirely new group of friends, and the bubble of romance and dependency would have burst.

But between the point where I accepted the scholarship and the point where I was actually supposed to go to college, I'd accumulated enough points playing pro tournaments to gain a ranking inside the top 100. I, and I alone, made the decision to forego the scholarship and devote my entire life to tennis. My reasoning was shortsighted, but logical. I thought that if I went to college, I'd have to start the whole process all over again. I remembered all of the satellite events in places like Olsztyn, Poland; and Tunis, Tunisia, that I'd had to play to get this far. I'd worked my entire life to play at the Grand Slam level, and now that I'd finally been given the opportunity, I didn't want to pass it up.

Had I possessed a greater belief in myself, I would have realized that I could have managed both college and a career, with a limited schedule of professional events that I could enter as an amateur. Had I been able to see the big picture, I also would have realized that a year in college would have been a valuable life experience, a dramatic and healthy departure from the one-dimensional life I'd lived until that point. However, since I had neither the confidence nor the foresight to choose the college path, I turned pro at age 18.

By committing to tennis at this point, I was also committing to Andrew. The next logical step was marriage. Aside from graduating from high school, my life hadn't changed all that much from when we'd first met: I lived with my parents, I played tennis, and I traveled with him. Even though I had occasional misgivings about committing myself so slavishly to this one sport, even after forgoing college, the whole arrangement was comfortable and predictable. In my young, relatively unformed mind, I would have been a fool to throw a wrench into this well-oiled machine.

Andrew and I got married in 1999, the same year I won Wimbledon with Lindsay, along with six other doubles titles. The wedding was another event in a year full of them, and the process of pulling it off seemed to take on an importance greater than why we were getting married in the first place. One hundred and forty people came, including my tennis friends such as Lindsay, Kim, and Lisa Raymond. After a dream honeymoon on St. Bart's, Andrew and I then returned home to our brand-new town house. I was finally out from under the constant gaze of my father and, for the first time, really on my own. Or so I thought.

As I suffered through the multiple rounds of chemo in the summer and fall of 2001, the assumption was that I'd probably never play tennis again. It wasn't anything that Andrew, my parents, or I discussed; it just struck us all as the inevitable price I'd have to pay for this awful disease. My husband and I began to prepare for a future that didn't involve my playing tennis or making the income I'd made from five years on the Tour. With his new job, Andrew could no longer drive me to Miami for regular chemo treatments. The upside was that he liked the job; the downside was that I spent a lot more time by myself.

The highlight of 2001 came between my second and third rounds of chemo. My sister-in-law, Laura, gave birth to a baby boy, Collin, on August 18. Fortunately, I was out of the hospital when Collin was due, and Mircea and Laura asked if I wanted to be present in the delivery room. I immediately accepted. Collin was my brother's first child, my parents' first grandchild, and my first nephew; and his arrival was a joyful distraction for all of us. Watching that baby come into this world was one of the most incredible experiences of my life—not only because I was in awe of the moment, but also because I felt extremely grateful to be alive to see it.

Soon after that blessed event, I was supposed to start my third course of chemo, but the USTA (United States Tennis Association) called the week before I was to begin to invite me to be their special guest at the U.S. Open in New York. It was a wonderful gesture, and I jumped at it. The idea was that I'd visit as a member of the family, so to speak, all expenses covered. My doctor allowed me to delay my chemo for two days, so I flew to New York. I was bald and extremely weak, but I was so excited by the prospect of being out of the land of cancer and back into the world of tennis.

It was another bittersweet event, to say the least. It was painful to see the women I'd competed against six months before and compare their health to mine. As *The New York Times* later described my appearance: "There was a bandanna covering Corina Morariu's head, leaden circles beneath her eyes and a pallid tint to her skin, all part of chemotherapy's cruel visuals." Meanwhile, the players were tan, fit, and running around, worrying about why they couldn't get a practice court at a certain time. It made me sad, but also a little angry. Many of their concerns now struck me as petty and irrelevant. I remember thinking, *I mean, does it really matter if you practice at 3:15 or 4:00? I have to go home in two days to get this poison injected into my bloodstream, so they can take me as close to dying as they can so that I can actually live. And you're worried because you can only get two cans of practice balls?*

This all came to a head one day when I was resting in the WTA office. A well-known player's mother, a woman I'd known for years, came in. She nodded to me in passing and then started complaining that she wasn't allowed to go into the locker room. The whole scenario was startling to me. I thought, *I'm the same age as your daughter, and all you can think about is access to the locker room?* At that moment, I was struck by what a self-absorbed existence I'd been leading in pursuit of a successful career in tennis. Six months before, *I* had been one of those players complaining about practice times and equipment. Now I was a cancer patient hoping and praying that I would survive the disease. Tennis is by nature a selfish enterprise because it has to be. Players are focused on themselves and what they must do to perform—and every need, want, or whim is catered to by those around them. But now that I was on the outside looking in, it seemed like a sudden, stark contrast from the new life I was living.

I went through a crazy range of emotions in those two days at the Open. I was an emotional tornado, fluctuating between happy and sad, grateful and angry, feeling sorry for myself and then snapping out of it to minimize my plight for the sake of others.

My third bout with chemo was scheduled to begin the day after I returned to Florida, and given my brief escape into the real world, it was especially difficult to go back to it. Driving home from the airport with Andrew, a song called "Superman" by Five for Fighting came on the radio. Tears started streaming down my cheeks as I listened to the lyrics, especially when the singer said that it wasn't easy to be him. That's exactly how I felt at that moment—it wasn't easy to be me.

BY THE TIME THE THIRD ROUND OF CHEMO DESTROYED my immune system again, my rectal pain had gone from bad to worse, and I spiked a fever once more, causing another admittance to the hospital. Not everyone gets an infection and a fever from chemo each time they undergo it, but I was batting a thousand.

I entered the hospital on September 9, 2001. As I was being admitted for what would be yet another two-week stay, I met a friendly, seemingly tight-knit family who appeared to recognize me. At that point I was probably at the height of my tennis-player-battling-cancer notoriety. There had been feature stories in *People, In Touch Weekly, Us Weekly* (as a reader myself, I got a perverse thrill out of being profiled in this gossip-magazine trifecta), and *USA Weekend,* among other mass-market magazines. We exchanged pleasantries and they followed me into the bone-marrow unit, where their son, Anthony, was being treated. I didn't know much more about them than that.

On September 11, I received a phone call from my mom, who was at home recovering from a hysterectomy. She told me to turn on the TV, as millions of Americans were doing at the exact same time. Her own set wasn't working, so I described the events to her while they were happening, something that made the horror that much more immediate. Having nothing to do in the hospital but stay glued to the television, I watched the story unfold for the next week, learning the fate of many of the victims along the way.

Meanwhile, I would occasionally ask the nurses how Anthony was doing and get minimal information in return. The night of the 9/11 telethon ten days later, when the whole nation was in mourning, a nurse told me that Anthony's health had deteriorated to the point that he'd been transferred to the ICU (intensive care unit). The bone-marrow unit itself was considered critical care, so I knew this was a terrible sign. It was at that moment that I learned his actual diagnosis: aplastic anemia. Back in May, this deadly disease was one of the possibilities for my own diagnosis. I instantly thought, *That could have been me,* and began sobbing uncontrollably. I was overwhelmed by the sadness and negativity of everything surrounding me, from my cancer and the horrors of 9/11 to this young kid dying in the ICU. I couldn't make sense of any of it. At that moment, it simply seemed as if there was nothing good in the world.

I called my brother, crying, and he started sobbing as well. Mircea was feeling guilty and apologized for not being there with me, even though his absence was completely understandable—he had both a new baby and a medical practice to handle. I got my evening's dose of Demerol and stopped crying immediately. The Demerol not only numbed the physical pain, but the emotional pain as well. Looking back on those long hospital stays in the bone-marrow unit spent alone with my thoughts, I realize that I used the Demerol just as much to escape the psychological trauma of my reality as to escape the physical agony of my illness.

As I prepared to turn in, my brother unexpectedly walked in the door. He'd driven all the way from Boca Raton to be with me. At "Hi, cutie," and a kiss on the cheek, I started to smile. He spent the night and helped me work through my grief. Again, my shining knight had come to the rescue.

Anthony died shortly after from pneumonia and other complications stemming from treatment for aplastic anemia. He was 18 years old.

A COUPLE OF DAYS AFTER MIRCEA'S VISIT, I went home for another brief reprieve before my fourth and final chemo session. The routine was set by now: chemo, pain, fever, hospital. I ended up spending Thanksgiving at Jackson Memorial, away from my family, with only Andrew to share some traditional fixings my mother had sent along. I didn't have much appetite for turkey and gravy. I just wanted out—of everything. Out of the hospital, out of the disease, out of what my life had become. Time slowed to an exasperating crawl.

With each course of chemotherapy, I got progressively weaker, and by the time I was finally released for good, I felt like a shell of a person, both physically and emotionally. I was not prepared for these brutal aftereffects.

A couple of days after I returned home, I went out with my parents to Sunday brunch. This had long been one of my all-time favorite customs, and even though I had little appetite, I wanted to try eating anyway. More than anything else, I thought that it would symbolize a return to normalcy. I was wrong—it just made my "new normal" painfully obvious. Outside, I had to sit down halfway between the parking lot and the restaurant to recover from the exhaustion. Inside, I couldn't even get up from the table to cruise the buffet. It was unnerving, to say the least. I'd gone from an athlete in the prime of life to someone who couldn't walk from the dining table to the buffet.

As physically depleted as I was, I knew that I would recover in time. But mentally, I didn't know what was going to happen. I didn't feel particularly elated about finishing the chemo treatment; in fact, it was just the opposite. My life felt utterly desolate, as I was finally, inescapably, faced with the question: "What are you going to do now?"

My life had been turned completely upside down. The only job I had ever known wasn't exactly something I could simply slide back into. And tennis wasn't just my job—it was my life and my world. After all the chemo was over, I didn't have anything to keep me busy or occupy my mind. I'd answered the hundreds of fan letters and done all the interviews. Now I was in limbo; and I felt sad, lonely, isolated, and exhausted. At least emotionally, this state of uncertainty, weakness, and depression was worse than the cancer itself.

I felt like the chemo had not only killed the cancer cells, it had also killed my body and spirit. The deep exhaustion took a toll on my body, for sure, but the mental exhaustion of fighting this enemy day and night for the last eight months took a toll on my spirit. I didn't realize how much I'd been struggling until the whole treatment was over, and the fallout was devastating. I remember feeling as close to death in this post-cancer period as I did when I was first diagnosed with leukemia in May. I had no zest for life. I had no purpose. I had no future to conjure up. The same poison that had destroyed the leukemia had destroyed my very identity.

On top of it all, I felt guilty for feeling sorry for myself when I "should" have felt grateful to be alive. Still trying to be the perfect daughter/sister/wife, I tried to suppress my sadness and confusion as much as possible and not burden or upset anyone. I never thought of seeking psychological help, and no one in my family raised the prospect. Illness in a family of Eastern European doctors is very black and white: you're sick, and then, God willing, you get well again. The focus is on the medicine, not the psyche. When you've finally recovered, everything else will take care of itself. In retrospect, I wish that I *had* seen a therapist to help me through this dark passage, but I ended up keeping most of my anguish locked up inside.

My savior during all of this, as silly as it sounds, was a chocolate brown miniature dachshund puppy named Milo. Andrew and I decided that if I wasn't able to return to tennis and would be spending a large part of my days at home, we should get a dog. The moment Milo entered our lives, he gave me a purpose. He was my buddy and, in a way, my child. Already crate trained, when he needed to go in the middle of the night, he would wake me up, and I'd take him out. As I started feeling stronger, I'd take him to puppy kindergarten and train him by the hour. On those long afternoons of sleeping on the couch, completely drained of energy, Milo would sleep right next to me. With Andrew busy with his new job, Milo was my constant companion and principal source of happiness for a good six to eight weeks as I slowly regained my bearings.

And although no one close to me urged me to do so, I did eventually return to tennis. It was the same old game, but a whole new way of life.

• • • • • •

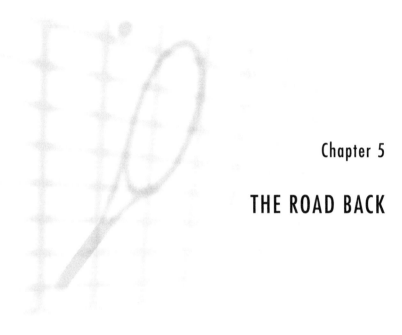

Chapter 5

THE ROAD BACK

By the middle of January 2002, I slowly began to feel better. An old friend named Philip Farmer was coaching tennis player Andrew Painter at the time, and he called to say that he was coming to South Florida. Philip had coached Tara Snyder, whom I'd played against in the pros, so I knew him well. When Philip arrived, his housing situation fell through, so I invited both men to stay with my husband and me. They were fun, upbeat guys who injected a much-needed jolt of lightheartedness into my life.

Before long, I was getting out of the house and wandering over to the courts to watch them practice. I was wearing a skirt and flip-flops the day Philip finally coaxed me into hitting a few balls. Swinging the racket took more effort than I could ever remember. I felt weak and completely inept, and after three minutes, I called it a day. But the seed was planted.

My husband, Andrew, and I had never really discussed whether or not I should attempt to play again—or if I *did* play, whether or not he should continue to be my coach. After all, he had a new coaching job that he enjoyed. Plus, in the past we'd made an effort to separate our tennis and personal lives by building a wall between home and the court. When I was on the practice court with Andrew, it was all business, superserious. This was both a reflection of our pact and of the way I was raised to regard tennis. The idea, which was continually reinforced by my dad's stern, no-nonsense attitude, was not really to have fun. It was to be ruthless in the drive to achieve, to push oneself at every moment to get better.

When Philip came along and I felt those first stirrings of desire to play again, it seemed like a fresh start. He was funny, cheerful, and a great fit for me; so it wasn't a tough decision to make. Both Andrew and I saw this as a way to remove tennis from the heart of our relationship and just be husband and wife, something we'd never really experienced before the cancer. I remember the day on the practice court when Andrew casually turned to Philip and asked, "So, what do you think about coaching my wife?" Philip's response was: "Are you kidding?"

On the occasion of my nephew's baptism, with the whole family gathered around, I made the big announcement that I was going to play tennis again. Everyone, including my father, was excited, although I truthfully don't think any of them really cared at that point. They were just happy that I was alive, so whatever I wanted to do was fine with them.

I realized that the situation had changed radically, at least in my own attitude toward playing. I now had a coach who worked strictly for *me,* and who had no ties or obligations to my family. I was free to pursue the game in any fashion I desired. If I just wanted to play for the fun of it, so be it. The leukemia, in a sense, had broken that inextricable, lifelong link between my family and tennis. Not only was my father now on the outside looking in—more spectator than taskmaster and disciplinarian—so was my husband. It was my decision to play, and mine alone. And I'd never really felt that way before, even when I chose to turn pro. I had always felt that I was playing to please someone else, to live up to their image of me as an athlete and a person.

For the next two months I willed my weak, atrophied body back into playing shape. I'd go to the gym daily and walk very slowly on the treadmill, a scarf still around my barren scalp. It's hard to describe the painful physical and mental transition I went through. As an athlete, I was used to working out in some form for five or six hours a day. Now, as a cancer survivor, I barely had the strength to walk. It was difficult to reconcile the two images of myself. I had so closely identified with my body for most of my life that I felt less like myself because I was such a weakling. But I still had the discipline and *determination* of an athlete. On the treadmill, I pushed myself every day to do a little more. As my hair grew, so did my strength. The day I finally ran half a mile at six miles an hour on the treadmill, I rushed to call Andrew. It was an exhilarating moment—I was on my way back.

BY THE END OF MARCH, I WAS FINDING MY FORM and hitting with friends on a regular basis. At a big pro tournament in Key Biscayne, Florida, Kim Po came to stay with Andrew and me while she played, and I began to hit with someone at my own pre-cancer level. I then spent two weeks in Dallas, where Philip lived, and had one of the best times of my new tennis life. We were working hard but also playing hard. Philip is only a couple of years older than I am, as are his friends, and hanging out with people close to my own age away from a tennis court was a whole new experience for me. It gave me a feeling of independence, something I imagine most young people feel when they first go off to college. I had flown the coop, so to speak.

I was thrilled at this point, feeling grateful for every moment. I appreciated what my body had once done and what it had just been through. I could almost feel the blood coursing through my veins as my strength returned. I got out of bed every morning and thought, *So this is what it feels like to be alive, to be human again.*

At the same time, I was faintly aware (and becoming more so all the time) of a serious underlying problem I was refusing to address: my marriage. I felt that I was having way too good of a time being away from my home and my husband. I was out every night, meeting new people, losing myself in an entirely new social world, and thinking little about my life back in Boca.

While I was away, Andrew and I entered a state of noncommunication about anything but the most mundane "How's your backhand?" topics. After what we'd both been through during the previous year, any admission that our marriage was on shaky ground was too scary to contemplate. Even making such an admission to myself made me feel like a selfish ingrate. Andrew had never wavered in his love and support of me through the worst crisis of my life, and he had both the deep affection and undying gratitude of my entire family. How could I even think of abandoning him after all that?

The truth—which slowly surfaced over the next six or seven months—was that Andrew and I had a relationship, before and during our marriage, that was completely intertwined with tennis. I had been a teenager when we'd first met—a teenager completely obsessed with tennis—and I'd had few boyfriends before him. I'd hardly been away from him, mentally or physically, since he'd become my full-time coach. Except when I was actually on the court playing, we spent virtually every moment together.

My husband and I were different in age, temperament, outlook, and even cultural signposts. We had different tastes in music, film, and fashion—we were of two different generations, really. Tennis was our primary means of contact and communication, the bridge that connected the two of us. After the leukemia completely ruptured my life, I felt that bridge start to crumble. Yet I wasn't fully conscious of this at the time; I only had a kind of disturbing inkling about the whole arrangement.

For Valentine's Day, I'd given Andrew the present of a trip home to Australia to see his family. He was planning to go for two weeks until I insisted that he stay for three. While he was gone in May, Philip came to Boca to work with me, but we had to suspend the workouts because I started having pain in my shoulder. This was the beginning of a long physical ordeal. Whether or not they were caused by my bout with cancer, from that point on, shoulder problems plagued me for the rest of my career.

After Philip returned to Dallas, I remember driving to the airport to pick up Andrew and feeling like the weight of the world was upon me. My heart was heavy with sadness and regret. It was such an awful emotional predicament, especially after years of being together with this man. I didn't feel angry or hateful or resentful or any other "hard" feelings; I just felt confused and riddled with guilt.

My way of dealing with these feelings was simply not to—I continued to suppress them and concentrate on my conditioning. I'd decided in the spring to start my comeback by playing World Team Tennis, which I signed up for in June.

Team Tennis is a commercial tennis competition that was initiated in 1974 to create a yearly event for pros completely outside of the traditional WTA or ATP (Association of Tennis Professionals) Tour. The format includes a 14-match summer season with teams from different cities made up of four players—two men and two women. A Team Tennis match involves five one-set events: men's singles, women's singles, men's doubles, women's doubles, and mixed doubles. Many great players have played in the league over the years, including John McEnroe, Jimmy Connors, and Billie Jean King, to name a few. When I was selected to join in 2002, I became a member of the Philadelphia Freedoms. Our coach was Mike DePalmer, and our theme song was written as a favor to Billie Jean by none other than Elton John and Bernie Taupin.

Team Tennis was the perfect transition for my way back into full-time professional tennis. It was great for the league because it could be promoted as my official comeback to the game. For me, it worked out well because it consisted of exhibition matches without ranking points or prize money on the line. I could gauge my performance against elite players in an atmosphere that minimized the stress on my body and mind. The short one-set matches didn't require long, extended periods of concentration or physical exertion.

To prepare for the Team Tennis season, I had to intensify my training. I went back to Dallas and started a rigorous routine of two long practice sessions, plus full practice matches, a day. At the same time, I reveled in the prospect of being away from home and on the road for much of the summer . . . although I refused to address why I was so ecstatic about this. I felt so incredibly guilty about my new attitude toward Andrew, a good man who had done nothing to push me away.

I remember my mother sitting me down during this period and telling me that she was worried about me. I think she sensed that I was having too much fun with Philip and assumed something inappropriate was going on between us. I reassured her, in no uncertain terms, that absolutely nothing was going on. "Do you really think," I asked, "that I would leave Andrew after everything he did for me when I was sick?"

Mom's instincts were right, though, at least about a growing rift between my husband and me. But since I wasn't about to acknowledge it, I bent over backward to alleviate her anxiety. I knew that to her and my father—and, in fact, my whole family—the mere possibility that I might break up with Andrew would cause an enormous amount of distress.

I STARTED PLAYING FOR THE FREEDOMS IN MID-JULY. Those 14 matches—in a hectic, compressed three-week schedule in cities from Philadelphia, Pennsylvania; to Newport Beach, California—were probably the most fun I ever had playing tennis. I was in my element. I was on a team with wonderful, high-spirited players: former #1 men's doubles player Jonathan Stark ("Starky"); South African Jessica Steck; and then 20-year-old, Brooklyn-born Levar Harper-Griffith. I was playing hard, but the matches weren't do-or-die. And the reception from the press and fans was phenomenal.

"Morariu Expects to Return From Leukemia," announced *The New York Times.* The article also mentioned my new coach and quoted me as saying that Andrew and I had "had nine months just being husband and wife . . . I enjoyed him being my husband." The headline in *The Philadelphia Inquirer* announced: "She's in Remission and on a Mission!" and stylishly reiterated that "after nearly a year spent locked in the phantom walls of the disease and within the real walls of the hospital, she was nearly where she was before." "A Champion Fights Back!" noted another newspaper, and I really felt like I *was* fighting back—and winning.

The crowds were great, averaging two thousand or more at some stops. People were constantly coming up to tell me what an inspiration I was, and I was just feeding off all the positive energy and thrilled to be playing again. My first singles match was against Amanda Coetzer, a former top-10 player. I was nervous as hell, this being my first competitive match since May 2001. Exhibition or not, I was still playing in front of a big crowd and wanted to do well for myself and my team.

On a good day, you can use a case of nerves to your advantage. The anxiety helps you focus and gives you a clear sense of the task at hand. That was exactly what happened—I won the one-set match, 5-1. Six hard months of retraining were paying off. I was completely in "the zone."

Team Tennis is sports entertainment, pure and simple. Music is played during the matches, creating a fun, lighthearted atmosphere for both the fans and the players. I loved a particular Eminem song at the time, "Without Me," and I remember hearing it blasting out of the loudspeakers during one of my singles sets. I immediately looked at my teammates on the bench and started dancing and laughing. I was absolutely having the time of my life, and my results showed it.

I was riding a wave and loving every minute of it until we arrived in Schenectady, New York, to play the team called the New York Buzz. By this point in the schedule, my shoulder pain had increased to the point that I needed to see a trainer before the match. Not only was my shoulder sore, my armpit was sore as well. After going over my history, the trainer told me that a sore armpit could be related to my lymph nodes and I should see a doctor immediately. I freaked. Was I having a relapse? Was another bout of cancer brewing? I immediately called my brother in tears from outside the trainer's trailer. In his calm, reassuring manner, Mircea told me not to worry, that my soreness could be related to any number of things. I went ahead and played the match, then went to see a doctor back in Philadelphia the next day. My blood work was fine. It was a complete false alarm.

This whole episode was indicative of how the cancer was still very much on my mind. The rule of thumb is that it takes five years for a cancer like mine to be considered cured. The chances of relapse decrease as time goes by, but I was only one year in remission and very cognizant of how I was feeling from day to day. The fear of a relapse was always in the back of my mind.

I was sore all around because I hadn't played competitively for more than a year; and although it was only exhibition tennis, Team Tennis had a rigorous, compacted schedule. I kept playing and finished the season, but unfortunately, my shoulder problems would only get worse.

MY PLAN FROM THE START WAS TO TRAIN WITH PHILIP, play a season of Team Tennis, and then cap my comeback with a return to the pro circuit. As a player coming back from an illness or an injury on the WTA

Tour, you're given a special ranking if you've been off the Tour for a minimum of six months. Your ranking in both singles and doubles is frozen at the point when you got injured or sick. Once you return, you have a certain number of tournaments—in my case, eight—in which you can use that special ranking to enter tournaments and achieve a new current ranking. Ranking points only stay on the computer for 52 weeks, and since I had been off the Tour for more than a year, I had no actual ranking, only my special ranking. It was like starting over again. I started 2001 ranked around 30 but had dropped to 58 when I got sick. I wasn't winning matches at the time because I was dealing with cancer. To maintain or eventually better that ranking, I had to carefully choose which eight tournaments I was going to play.

Nagging shoulder pain aside, I felt that I was ready to play on the Tour again after those three strenuous weeks of Team Tennis. My first tournament back on the circuit was the Acura Classic at the La Costa Resort and Spa near San Diego, at the end of July 2002. This fit my comeback schedule perfectly, coming right after the Team Tennis season ended. I chose to play my first tournament in doubles only, as another test of my endurance and concentration.

I'd begun 2001 winning the mixed-doubles title at the Australian Open, but by the end of the year (again largely due to the fatigue and subpar play brought on by the encroaching cancer), my doubles ranking had fallen to 20. I teamed up with my old friend and partner Kim Po, now Kim Po-Messerli, having married Oliver Messerli in 2001. We played two very accomplished players, Meghann Shaughnessy and Chanda Rubin, in the first round. Kim and I lost, but all things considered, I played well and felt good. It was a tough three-set match that was frustrating to lose, but my body had held up nicely, and that was my first priority.

"Smashing Return" read one headline. After our loss, the caption for the photo accompanying an AP article said: "Loss Can't Spoil Comeback." The article's lead paragraph began: "Corina Morariu was a winner just by playing in the first-round doubles of the Acura Classic." Having seen the reception I'd received during Team Tennis, I knew that playing again might benefit other people out there struggling with cancer. "If I can provide some strength or hope to others in the same situation," I'm quoted as saying, "then that is really important."

The next week I signed up for both singles and doubles at a tournament at the Manhattan Country Club in Manhattan Beach, California, another step toward returning to full strength. In my opening singles match, I was playing a young woman named Marie-Gayanay Mikaelian, who was ranked about 50 at the time. I started well, winning the first set and leading early in the second. Physically, I was clearly up to the task—but as the match progressed, I started to weaken mentally. Lacking psychological stamina, I slowly lost my concentration and made some costly mistakes. I ended up losing the last two hard-fought sets, 7-5 and 6-4.

Match tough is a term we tennis players use, and for all my progress in the last six or seven months, I had yet to become match tough again. There is nothing like the unflagging tension you feel when you're playing a match in front of a crowd, fighting for ranking points, money, and pride. You can practice all you want, but you can't duplicate the intensity and pressure of match play on a practice court. It governs not only how you swing the racket and place your shots, but also how you're processing the game in your mind, the chatter that goes on in the brain of every athlete.

The only possible way you can learn how to manage those emotions and maintain focus and concentration is to play point after point after point in a real match. It's like another muscle you can only exercise and train as you're actually playing. If you've been out of commission, as I had been, you have to relearn how to block out the chatter and pay total attention to every single point. This is tough even if you play all the time. Many pros go through lulls in matches where they seem to become distracted and lose touch with what they're doing. And that calls for yet another intangible skill: the ability to regain focus after losing it. It's all part of being match tough, and I wasn't quite there yet.

In doubles, Kim Po-Messerli and I won the first two rounds, which were the first wins of my comeback. Sadly, we lost in the semifinals to two accomplished players, Kim Clijsters and Jelena Dokic.

What's interesting is that no one in my family flew out to see me play in these first two pro tournaments, although it didn't strike me as either odd or distressing at the time. My return to tennis had been my choice, and I think that by this point, my parents felt as if they'd done all they could to see me through the leukemia and help me get back on my feet. They were in no way washing their hands of me—they were simply returning to their own lives after the constant strain of dealing with my circumstances for more than a year. In a way, it freed me to play on my own terms and critique my own performance.

I went back to Florida to rest and practice for what one might call the pivotal event of my comeback: the U.S. Open. This would be my first Grand Slam event since my decision to return to the game, a way of saying that not only had I survived, but I was ready to compete at the highest levels again.

I HAD TO GET ANOTHER BONE-MARROW TEST to make sure the cancer hadn't returned, meaning that I was practicing on one sore hip. And when the draw for the U.S. Open was announced, I got the unenviable slot playing Serena Williams, the number one player in the world at the time, in the first round. It was disappointing news to be sure, but no matter what the draw was, I was eager to get back on the court in New York.

Serena and I were scheduled to play that first match in Arthur Ashe Stadium on Monday night, following a ceremony that honored the victims of 9/11. As soon as we took the court, the crowd support was overwhelming. As one newspaper reported, there was "a crescendo of applause that was as much for [Morariu's] bravery in beating cancer as it was for Williams, the French Open and Wimbledon winner who has put a hammerlock on women's tennis."

Serena came out and immediately stunned the crowd (and me), before she'd even hit a ball. Prior to the match, she and I were waiting in the locker room, and I noticed that she was wearing a warm-up jacket and tight shorts—the kind that most female players wear *under* their skirts. As our match time approached, I kept wondering when Serena was going to put her skirt on (yes, these were my thoughts before one of the biggest matches of my career). She was still partially undressed three minutes before our scheduled match time.

I left the locker room a few minutes before she did to do my prematch interview. It wasn't until she walked onto the court that I realized she had no skirt! She dropped her warm-up jacket—and that's when we all saw that she was wearing a body-clinging, black faux-leather catsuit. It was one of the most outrageous fashion statements in the history of tennis. One commentator said that "it would have given members of the All England Club [that is, Wimbledon] heart palpitations."

I remember walking out on the court that night, just wanting to soak up the electrifying atmosphere. As *The New York Times* put it: "Morariu walked into Arthur Ashe Stadium to face the ferocity of Serena Williams with the upbeat attitude and sun-kissed look of a cruise director." I didn't exactly feel like a cruise director, but I did feel like a professional tennis player. The crowd was cheering loudly, and I felt a tremendous sense of pride. I'd worked so hard to get to this moment after the weak, pale, and bald condition I'd been in exactly one year before. To drive the point home, the networks kept showing split-screen images of my emaciated, wan, dealing-with-cancer look in 2001 and my healthy, tan, post-cancer look.

No matter how either of us looked or felt, Serena put her vaunted hammerlock on me that night. I was outmatched physically and lost to a better player—not to mention the fact that I still wasn't as match tough as I wanted to be. It was a challenge for me to maintain my focus and still retain my appreciation for the moment. I lost 6-3, 6-2, and although I was disappointed by how I played, I was grateful for the entire experience. (Serena went on to win the whole tournament, finally beating her sister Venus for the title.)

After the match, I wasn't the least bit glum at having lost so handily. "I didn't think last year at this time I'd be able to do this," I told the press that surrounded me. "I'm a lucky girl." Even my friends chimed in: "What really surprises me," Lindsay was quoted as saying in *The New York Times*, "is how great she looks. I remember being here at the Open last year and she had no muscle, obviously she had no hair, was very frail. You see her now, it almost seems like that didn't really happen to her last year. It's amazing." A headline from a local South Florida paper summed it all up: "She's Back in the Game."

Genuinely *feeling* back in the game, I decided to play both doubles and mixed doubles at the Open. I paired up in doubles with Kim Po-Messerli again, and we made a statement, if only a quiet one. We made it to the quarterfinals, beating the great team of Liezel Huber and Nicole Arendt along the way. And then, in mixed doubles, I made the spur-of-the-moment decision to team up with Justin Gimelstob.

I'D KNOWN JUSTIN ALL MY TENNIS LIFE, but this was the first time we'd be playing as a team. It turned out that we enjoyed playing together, and we made it to the semifinals (before losing to Mike Bryan and Lisa Raymond). More important, Justin and I reconnected for the first time since I'd gotten cancer.

We first met through Tim Gullikson, who was my coach, mentor, and role model for many years. By the time I first worked with Tim, he was an accomplished and celebrated coach. He'd already worked with stars such as Martina Navratilova and Mary Joe Fernandez, and he was soon to join forces with perhaps his most famous client: Pete Sampras. Tennis fans will never forget the moment during the 1995 Australian Open when Pete broke down in tears on the court while playing Jim Courier. He'd just found out that Tim was seriously ill, later to be diagnosed with a brain tumor. Tim Gullikson was deeply loved by everyone who knew or worked with him.

I began to work with this amazing man when I was only 11. We'd play at the local park or sometimes at my dad's club, an hour lesson at a time. Tim was perfect for me in so many ways. He was, first of all, a great escape from my father—my principal coach and taskmaster up to that point. Sometimes half of my lesson with Tim would be devoted to talking (and crying) about my decidedly mixed feelings about tennis before I finally got around to hitting balls. We used to joke that our practice time was half tennis lesson and half psychotherapy session. Tim enjoyed talking and never failed to make me laugh and feel better about my situation. I love my dad with all my heart, but Tim was so supportive and encouraging that he became almost a surrogate father figure in those preteen years.

Tim was also the only cancer victim I'd ever really known before I became one myself. He died from his brain tumor 16 months after being diagnosed, and his attitude throughout was nothing short of extraordinary. He was constantly upbeat and positive and never succumbed to self-pity or despair. As I lay in that hospital bed after the onset of leukemia, I thought of Tim often. I thought of his courage, perseverance, and cheerful manner in the face of his near-certain fate. Through his powerful example, he helped coach me through the toughest ordeal of my life.

Tim also used to coach Justin. Although he's just a year older than I am, Justin's parents would fly him down from New Jersey specifically to take lessons from Tim. I would have a lesson, and Justin would have the lesson before or after me, so we'd often run into each other and make small talk.

Justin and I grew up playing junior tennis together, constantly bumping into each other at various national tournaments and USTA training camps. Over the years we got to know each other quite well. I always had a soft spot for him, even though at an early age he'd developed the reputation of a temperamental bad boy who would go to any lengths to win a match. He was probably all that and more, but I saw a different side of him—someone with a good heart who was charming, sensitive, and very bright. And above all, he made me laugh. I have vivid memories of our days at USTA camps being doubled over with laughter at something he said or did.

In his pro career, Justin reached the rank of 63 as a singles player, won several doubles titles, and was a fierce competitor. But it was his quick wit and loud mouth that endeared him to many in the tennis world, yet irritated and offended many others. *The New York Times* once noted that "several female tennis stars" called Justin "a decent guy with some self-modulation issues," which is a kind way of saying that he occasionally said some colossally stupid things that got him in a lot of trouble. At one point, he was called the "Most Quotable Guy on the ATP Tour." He was very witty, razor sharp with the one-liners, and never hesitated to speak his mind. That was part of what I liked about him—he was complex, and you could never call him boring.

During that U.S. Open that reintroduced me to the larger tennis public, Justin and I were no more than doubles partners and old tennis friends. And we remained "just friends" for a long time after that. But as my tennis career rebounded and my personal life began to disintegrate into an agonizing mess, pitting me against almost everyone in my immediate family, Justin was there for me at every turn in the road.

• • • • • •

With my older brother, Mircea, and our father outside our house in Bloomfield Hills, Michigan. Dad would play tennis with Mircea, and they'd often take me along.

At 18 months, I was already used to having a racket nearby.

In my full getup, going to play my first tournament at age six. I'm trying to put on a brave face, but I was so nervous I think I was just trying not to throw up.

Playing in one of my earliest tournaments.

In my favorite tennis outfit with my parents, celebrating my dad's birthday.

My first Fed Cup in Madrid, Spain, 1998. *From left:* Lisa Raymond; Monica Seles; our captain, Billie Jean King; Mary Joe Fernandez; and me. I still feel that being named to the U.S. Fed Cup team was one of my greatest accomplishments as a player. I loved team competition and felt honored to represent my country, and some of my fondest memories come from my time on this team.

Lindsay Davenport and me after winning Wimbledon in 1999. She'd won the singles title earlier that day, and I remember thinking how great it was that she seemed equally excited about winning the doubles. *(Courtesy of Getty Images)*

Playing Lindsay at Wimbledon's Centre Court in 2000. I would fall and break my arm later in this very match. *(Courtesy of Getty Images)*

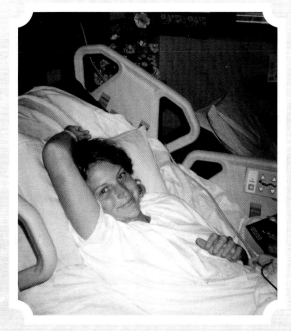

At Jackson Memorial Hospital, May 2001, right after I was diagnosed with acute promyelocytic leukemia. This was at the beginning of my monthlong stay.

With my two constant companions at Jackson: my brother, Mircea (left); and my husband at the time, Andrew. My room was full of balloons from friends, family, and fans. The outpouring of support meant more to me than words could ever express.

Andrew holding me up on my ten-minute field trip outside, the only time I would get to go outdoors during my hospitalization.

"Before"—my hair had been falling out for days, and it was looking pretty straggly when I finally mustered up the courage to have my brother cut it all off.

"During"—Mircea's idea of a joke while shaving my head. Judging by the huge smile on my face, he clearly wasn't the only one who thought my intermediate coif was pretty funny. We really did try to find humor in everything.

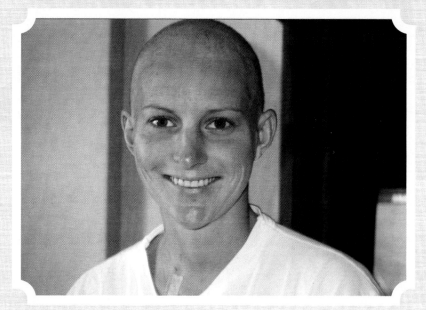

"After"—bald, but still smiling. If losing my hair meant I had a chance to live, that was fine by me.

These bandanas, modeled by Mircea and me, were gifts from my friends Lisa Raymond and Rennae Stubbs. They were certainly put to good use.

With my first nephew, Collin, right after he entered the world on August 18, 2001. His birth was the happiest moment of that difficult year, and I was so grateful that I got to be in the room to witness it.

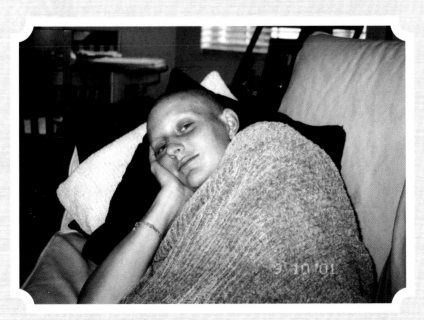

September 2001, on my couch, where I'd spend most of my time in between hospital stays.

A year after going to the U.S. Open in between chemo treatments, I was back playing at Arthur Ashe stadium against Serena Williams. *(Courtesy of Getty Images)*

Starting my comeback in 2002, here I am playing doubles with my good friend Kim Po-Messerli. *(Courtesy of Getty Images)*

With my family in 2004. *From left:* my sister-in-law, Laura; Dad; Mom; me; and my brother, Mircea.

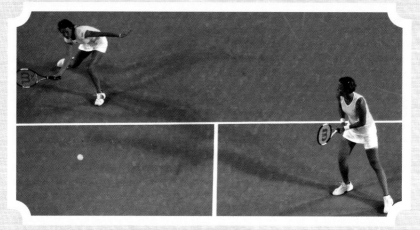

Playing in the finals of the Australian Open with Lindsay, January 2005.
(Courtesy of Getty Images)

Lindsay and me, teary-eyed after our speeches, with our runner-up trophies at the Australian Open. Even though we'd lost the match, I still considered the whole experience a victory. I stood on that court as a cancer survivor, grateful to play another Grand Slam final and proud that I'd accomplished something postcancer that I'd achieved *before* I was diagnosed with leukemia. *(Courtesy of Getty Images)*

In Delray Beach, Florida, for the 2005 Fed Cup. *From left:* Venus Williams; our captain, Zina Garrison; me; Serena Williams; and Lindsay. *(Courtesy of Getty Images)*

With Rennae Stubbs after we won in Sydney in 2006. It was my first title after beating cancer. *(Courtesy of Getty Images)*

Lindsay and me at the Four Seasons in Bali. We played the 2006 tournament there and won our last title together, but we used the trip as a working vacation.

With Raj—my coach, friend, and mentor throughout the toughest years of my life. This picture was taken on the day I retired from professional tennis in 2007. Note the huge smile on my face!

With my nephews, Collin and Chet, otherwise known as "my happy place."

In 2008, at my new job commentating for Tennis Channel. *(Courtesy of Cameraworksusa)*

In the booth with Justin at the 2009 Australian Open in Melbourne, just before we called a match together.

Working at the 2009 U.S. Open, interviewing the women's singles champ, Kim Clijsters. *(Courtesy of Cameraworksusa)*

Chapter 6

BACK ON TOUR

After the 2002 U.S. Open, I rested my shoulder briefly, and then went on a three-week swing through Asia to play some smaller tournaments. They were still Tour-level events, but given their size, I thought they might provide the opportunity to play more matches and increase my level of match toughness. At the same time, I could work on building my new ranking. Frankly, the draws here would be a little easier than the Serena-level draws of the big summer tournaments.

Before I left, I made the decision to part ways with Philip as my coach. Although he had certainly helped me get back into playing shape and have a little more fun with the game, the chemistry wasn't quite right for a long-term partnership in ongoing tournament play.

My first stop was Hawaii, where I won my first-round match—my first post-cancer singles win. Even though I then lost to Cara Black, the woman who ended up winning the tournament, I felt optimistic about my game. I was getting better with every match and was now confident that I could play competitively day in and day out.

Andrew was with me on this trip to Hawaii, but neither of us was ready for him to reassume the role of coach in my life. I played that particular tournament without a formal coach but knew I needed to find one to continue my progress. My friend Lisa Raymond suggested a guy she knew named Raj Chaudhuri. Raj had worked with Lisa on the Fed Cup team shortly after my first stint on the team.

Of Indian parentage, Raj had been raised in the Midwest. He'd played tennis in college and a little on the Tour, and he was currently building his reputation as a coach. Now, with Andrew standing right there, I practiced with him a couple times to feel him out. Raj later told me that he felt like he was being tested in front of Andrew. Well, he passed the test—both my husband and I thought he'd be a great fit. Andrew then headed back to the States, feeling good about my situation.

Raj and I went on to the next tournament in Bali, where my dad joined me. It was the first time either of my parents had watched me play since my battle with leukemia. Dad now came to a couple of practices but in no way interfered. It was clear that, post-cancer, his involvement in my tennis life was over.

As for Raj, he was exactly the right coach at the right time. For one thing, he had a completely fresh view of my tennis strengths and weaknesses. But more than his knowledge of the game and his approach to technique, what set him apart was his entire approach to playing. More than anyone I had ever worked with, Raj focused as much on my attitude and mind-set as he did on the arc of my swing. In a way, he reminded me of my early interactions with Tim Gullikson, where I would spend an equal amount of time playing and talking about my life. It was the same with Raj—we talked as much as we hit balls. He constantly encouraged me to be more introspective and more honest with myself. And, most important, he made tennis fun.

"Honestly, I tell you this all the time, Corina," he later stated. "One of my most gratifying moments as a coach was the time we were working together after a couple months of work, and you turned to me and said, 'You know, I really enjoyed that today.' You said it with such surprise in your voice. I asked, 'Is this new?' And you said, 'I've never actually enjoyed practice.' I said, 'Ever?' 'No, never,' you replied. 'It's something I do, but today I got a kick out of it.' I thought it was amazing that you were so good and had gotten so far, but only now realized there was some joy to be had—and you hadn't had a piece of it yet."

At the tournament in Bali, I won my first round. Then, early in the second round, my shoulder totally gave out. I retired from the match and told Raj that it was time for me to go home and take care of my body. I was scheduled to play another tournament in Asia, but I had to withdraw. I was disappointed and demoralized. I'd been trying to build some momentum, but with the Tour about to end for the year, I wasn't going to get enough matches in to build either my endurance, my confidence, or my ranking. I went home to nurse my wounds.

RIGHT AROUND THAT TIME, I RECEIVED A CALL FROM JOHN ARRIX, the director of the WTA Tour Championships, one of the most prestigious events on the calendar. The WTA had created an annual award in my honor, called the Corina Morariu Courage Award, and they wanted me to be the first recipient. The event that year was to be played at the Staples Center in Los Angeles. Would I be willing to fly out to accept the award?

Absolutely.

The Tour Championships take place at the end of each season and only include the year's eight top singles players and the four top doubles teams. Given the level of play, it's almost like a fifth Grand Slam for women. Lindsay and I qualified as a doubles team for the Championships in 1999 and played at Madison Square Garden in New York, another one of the highlights of my career. The year of the inaugural Courage award, the best women players included the Williams sisters, Jennifer Capriati, Kim Clijsters, and Monica Seles, among others.

I was more than flattered that someone thought I deserved to have the word *courage* inscribed on an award next to my name. Courage, to me, is perseverance in the face of adversity, something many people quietly go about exhibiting every day. I knew that surviving cancer and returning to tennis required will and determination, but I never thought of it as courageous. It's a powerful word, *courage,* and it took me a while to believe that I'd actually shown some by not letting fear, pain, or doubt deter me from coming back. I finally came to appreciate the award as a well-timed culmination of 18 months of blood (literally), sweat, and tears.

I took one of my best friends in the world—my mother—to L.A. in November to attend the various ceremonies. There was a pre-tournament dinner at the Fairmont Miramar Hotel & Bungalows in Santa Monica, attended by all the players. Lindsay introduced me to the gathering, and when I got up to speak, I was overcome by emotion. I can't remember exactly what I said, but I do remember, vividly, how I felt. I cried tears of joy and gratitude, feeling not only incredibly thankful to be alive, but also greatly appreciative for the enormous outpouring of love and support the event epitomized.

I also saw quite a bit of Justin while I was in L.A. for what turned into a weeklong vacation with my mom. He and I had stayed in touch since playing together in the U.S. Open, and he drove down to Hermosa Beach to see me at Kim's house when we first arrived. A few days later, he was to pick me up at my hotel in Santa Monica so we could find a cake to celebrate Kim's recent retirement. I waited outside. No Justin. It wasn't entirely unusual for him to be late, but after a half-hour, I started to worry. A few minutes later, I got a call from him, and his opening line was: "Now it's your turn to visit *me* in the hospital." We'd laugh about the irony of that comment for years because he had never actually come to visit me in the hospital. But I was too worried to think about that at the time.

It turns out that Justin had been out riding his bike that morning and had been hit by a car. I rushed to the hospital to find him with a few staples in his head and some bumps and bruises, but not in mortal danger. I helped him through the day, and we spent the next eight hours together, mixing sarcasm with tender recollections of our years of friendship. There is no question that the experience of that day strengthened our bond.

In front of a large crowd at the Staples Center a couple nights later, I formally received the first Corina Morariu Courage Award. Justin made it, injuries and all—as did Kim and her husband, Oliver; and, of course, my mom, seated front and center. I accepted the award on behalf of all the people battling a disease like leukemia without the public support and encouragement I had received. They were quietly dealing with this horrible circumstance away from headlines and crowds, and they deserved recognition for their courage as well. The evening ended with a little party at the hotel, where we toasted both Kim's retirement and my award. It was a celebration of life and friendship, a perfect ending to a momentous occasion.

AFTER THAT WONDERFUL EVENT IN L.A., IT WAS TIME TO FACE FACTS: I needed to deal with my recurring shoulder problems. Justin had known about them since we'd played together at the Open, and he offered to help. He announced, in his typical take-charge manner, that he was going to arrange for me to see former Davis Cup doctor David Altchek in New York.

Justin had played on the Davis Cup team in both 1998 and 2001, so he had an entrée with this noted orthopedic surgeon and sports-medicine specialist. At that point, I was willing to do anything to fix my shoulder, so I jumped at the chance. Justin was planning on visiting his parents in New Jersey about the same time, so he offered to accompany me to the appointment. It sounded like a plan.

I flew to New York, having been invited by Justin's parents to stay at their home. Justin and I drove into the city to see Dr. Altchek the next day. After evaluating me, he announced that he thought I'd torn my labrum (cartilage in the upper part of the scapula). He'd need me to get an MRI to be sure, but this type of injury to the shoulder generally required arthroscopic surgery.

Justin stayed with me the entire time, through the MRI and then back to Dr. Altchek's office where the initial diagnosis was confirmed. I needed surgery, but Dr. Altchek couldn't schedule the procedure for a few weeks. No shrinking violet, Justin jumped in and said, "Oh, come on, doc—what about next week?" The doctor agreed to do the operation on Monday, three days later, just before Thanksgiving. In his bullish yet charming way, my friend had accelerated the process and made my life much easier.

I stayed at Justin's parents' home that weekend and went in for arthroscopic surgery on Monday morning. Afterward, the doctor came to see me in the recovery room. He told me that the problem he fixed was not as bad as he'd originally thought. He was perplexed by my level of pain, because it didn't fit with the damage he'd seen in my shoulder. Regardless, the procedure was finished, and I could soon begin rehab on the area and eventually return to play.

Looking back, it was odd that Andrew and I never discussed his coming to New York and helping me through this. He didn't offer, and I didn't ask; it just never came up. My mom was pressing to be with me, but I simply wanted to be on my own. She fought me on it, but finally got the point and backed off.

During this whole episode, I realized that I was seeing a different side of Justin than I'd ever seen before. My general attitude toward him, dating back years, was that he had a good heart and could make me laugh, but he could be self-centered and mercurial. Over the course of those few days, I saw that he wasn't so narcissistic. He took care of me, not out of any obligation, but strictly out of concern. When I came out of surgery, he was right there by the bed, flipping through magazines, telling jokes and making fun of my loopy, drug-induced state. And when I'd sufficiently recovered, he drove me back to New Jersey and put me to bed in the room next to his. It was all very sweet.

The next night he went out on a date, and when he returned, he came into my room with a major announcement: he was in love with me. I was floored. I'd started feeling closer to him through this trip, but he wasn't talking "closer." Justin was pouring his heart out

It was an intense, deeply vulnerable, and audacious display. It was also the most passionate outpouring of emotion I had ever witnessed. After a long night of confession, Justin had certainly made his point. Yet although I was deeply touched, I wasn't about to fall into his arms.

The next morning, he drove me to the airport, visibly upset. The situation was surreal, and I didn't really know what to say. I hadn't told anyone that I was unhappy in my marriage; in fact, I had yet to even admit it to myself. I couldn't commit to Justin in any way, and he knew that.

Recognizing the futility of the situation, Justin stopped talking to me during the ride to Newark. Then when he dropped me off, he told me that he could no longer be in contact with me because it would be too painful for him. I was not to call him, and he was certainly not going to call me. I was crestfallen. I felt that Justin and I were becoming good friends for the first time in our long acquaintance, but he wasn't looking for friendship at that point. After his prolonged emotional outpouring, I could completely understand how he felt.

AFTER I BOARDED THE PLANE, I SAT THERE waiting for takeoff with everything swirling around in my mind at once. I was trying to process it all: Justin's overpowering feelings, my marriage, recovering from cancer, playing pro tennis again, just having shoulder surgery—all of the life-changing events of the past year. I wasn't ready to tell him this, but I definitely felt something for Justin, and I'd realized this even before he confessed his feelings. This wasn't the first time I'd felt this kind of attraction since the cancer. I had never acted upon it, and I don't think I even realized it was happening at the time. But now, as I sat on that plane, I realized one thing clearly: I was deeply estranged from my husband. In my mind, I was not acting the way a married woman should have been acting. Something was either seriously wrong with *me* or my marriage (quite possibly both).

I thought about the new home Andrew and I had purchased. We'd bought it in January before it had been built, and we moved in right before I took off for this fateful trip to New York. The house had been a great source of distraction for the year—Andrew and I could spend hours discussing "important" matters like bathroom tile and kitchen countertops, avoiding more uncomfortable topics such as the growing chasm between us. I realized now that we must have hoped this house would somehow fix everything between us. I think that on some level we both knew our marriage was crumbling, but it was just too frightening to admit. Lighting fixtures were much easier to discuss.

Now as I sat on that plane, I would have given just about anything to avoid going back to Boca Raton, where my husband, a new home, and Thanksgiving with my family awaited me. I wanted to go see friends in L.A., play a tennis tournament in China, fly to the moon—I didn't really care. The idea of resuming the life I'd lived more or less since age 15—the compliant daughter, sister, and wife—was too much to accept. This was not the way I should have been thinking, feeling, or behaving. But I had reached a tipping point and absolutely knew, at that very moment: *I can't do this anymore.*

All the signs now pointed in the same direction: there was either something seriously wrong with me, or something seriously wrong with my marriage. I hadn't come to terms with the situation until that very moment. As soon as I admitted the truth to myself, I was hit with a flood of emotions: Guilt. Regret. Sadness.

I remember getting off the plane and meeting Andrew, and I instantly felt like I was going to throw up, either from the shoulder pain or the awkwardness of the situation (or, most likely, both). I'd left with one suitcase and returned with two, the second one for a Cryo Cuff used to ice my shoulder. Andrew made some passing quip about the two bags, and I snapped. It wasn't what I said; it was the nasty way I said it. I'll never forget how hurt he looked at that moment. I was equally taken aback by the hostility in my voice. I was obviously really mad at *myself* and the whole untenable situation, rather than angry at my husband.

Once I arrived home, I immediately popped a couple of Percocets like M&M's. I would like to say that I took the painkillers that day to ease my aching shoulder, but the truth is that I used them to escape my oppressive reality. The fact that I happened to arrive home on the day of our third wedding anniversary didn't seem to matter to either of us. Neither of us had gotten the other a gift or flowers or even thought about a romantic evening together. I simply hid out in plain sight.

THE NEXT DAY WAS THANKSGIVING, SO THE BOYS—Andrew, Mircea, and my dad—went out to play a round of golf while Mircea's wife, Laura, and I stayed back to prep the big dinner. That morning, Laura was the first person in the family I openly admitted my unhappiness to. This was slightly strange, since we weren't exactly confidantes. We'd grown much closer since the big family feud at Wimbledon in 1999, but we still weren't intimate secret sharers. I decide to tell her first because I thought she'd understand my state of mind. I made a good choice.

Laura was my sounding board that day, and for many days after, but she also helped me understand my situation even more clearly. As she said at the time, "You've been so completely sheltered for so many years that you don't even *know* you've been sheltered." In a very short time, I'd gone from being a young girl to getting sick and almost dying . . . to becoming an adult. Like my father and brother before him, Andrew served as my caretaker. And I didn't need or want a caretaker anymore. It was as simple, and as emotionally wrenching, as that.

Laura later liked to use the analogy of the glass ceiling to explain what happened. My own glass ceiling wasn't some artificial sexist limitation on what I could achieve as an athlete. It was an *emotional* glass ceiling that kept me bound by the decisions other people made for me in my life, along with my own acceptance of those decisions. My bout with cancer had shattered that illusion of dependence, and I'd become a completely different person with different needs and a different sense of self.

Before the big dinner that day, I also called Kim in L.A. to explain the situation. My friends in tennis had no doubt seen this coming: They'd all seen Andrew and me together for years, and it never made sense to any of them. They didn't see the relationship as mean or abusive; I wasn't married to a philanderer or a drug addict. They just saw it as dysfunctional, that we were an odd couple not exactly suited to each other. Although I was calling Kim, what I really wanted to do was get on a plane and go see her. For whatever reason, I was being pulled west. I wanted to get away from my family, Andrew, Justin— *everything*—and find a safe place to regain my equilibrium.

Somehow I made it through Thanksgiving dinner. When it was over, and my parents and Andrew were in the other room, I told Mircea how I felt. I couched it in the softest language possible: "I'm not happy." His response was: "I know." That struck me. I thought I'd been doing a great job of hiding my unhappiness, but at least with Mircea, someone who could read me as well as anyone, I had failed. He didn't get outwardly angry with me, but he certainly didn't rush to my defense either.

I went home that same night and finally told Andrew what I was really feeling. I think I used the same words with him that I'd used with my brother, but my recollection of the whole conversation is fuzzy at best. It was such a surreal moment—a fateful moment—that I don't think I really knew what I was saying as I was saying it. I had a pit in my stomach, a tightening that would not go away, and one that would be with me for months. I was stepping into emotional territory that was foreign and frightening to me. I might have known in my heart that our marriage was over for some time, but I hadn't been ready to admit it, even in my most private thoughts.

Andrew didn't get angry or overly emotional. While he was quiet and generally tranquil by nature anyway, at that point he was probably more stunned than anything. *I* didn't fully grasp what I was saying, so how could I expect *him* to? Understandably, he went into "Let's fix it" mode. He turned the discussion to finding someone who might be able to help us deal with our problems. Eventually, he made a call to my cousin's wife, Katia Deac, who was a psychiatrist. The next logical step was counseling.

Over coffee the next morning, I told my dad that I'd reached a crisis point in my marriage. Like Andrew, he really didn't know what to say. He didn't explode or attack me in any way—he, too, was in shock. I tried to explain my feelings about the situation, but I don't think he understood. My guess is that he didn't even understand why I was telling him this in the first place. I was unhappy? So what? I was married, and everyone in a marriage goes through periods when they're unhappy. That's life.

It took some time for my father's feelings to gel, but in his own words, both he and my mother became "very, very, very upset." I didn't realize exactly *how* upset he would become as time went on, probably because I saw it as my problem and my decision to make, not something that everyone else in the family would feel was their problem or responsibility to fix.

As the crisis unfolded, I realized that I could not have been more wrong.

• • • • • •

Chapter 7

WORSE THAN LEUKEMIA

From the moment I announced to Andrew that I was unhappy in our marriage, I knew I was in the fight of my life. It was essentially four against one, with Laura being the only sympathetic ear in my camp. The rest of the family indeed fought me all the way, sometimes loudly, sometimes simply with disappointing looks. I knew intuitively that I wasn't happy, but there was so much more to it than that that it was difficult for me to sift through my feelings. There were the emotions underlying my now-public estrangement from my husband—guilt, relief, anger, defiance—compounded by the emotions behind my illness, my injury, and my career uncertainty. It felt like everything was coming at me at once.

Like my mom and dad, my brother was blindsided by what unfolded over the next couple of months. Mircea and my parents are Catholics and hold to the traditional belief that couples marry for life. Our own parents hadn't exactly had an easy marriage, as both will readily admit, but they'd never split up. Andrew had clearly not caused my disillusionment by any overt act. On the contrary—he had fulfilled every one of my family's prerequisites for being a good husband. Mircea also saw Andrew as my protector, which was the role my brother had played my whole life. Mircea and Andrew are about the same age, so it's easy to understand how he could see Andrew stepping in and taking over his brotherly/fatherly role for me. He came to love Andrew like his own brother and completely trusted him to do the right thing. As Mircea later said, "I didn't have to worry about you dating numskulls and idiots."

He went on to explain how he felt during this time: "It was brutal. Someone very close to me, my *actual* sibling, was breaking up with someone else very close to me, my *virtual* sibling. I couldn't exactly tell you you were wrong for feeling that Andrew wasn't the one for you for the long term, though. I'd told you in the beginning, when you said you were about to get married, that you didn't have enough life experience to make a decision like that."

If I'd listened to Mircea in the first place, I wouldn't have been in the mess I was now in, and here I was, ignoring his advice once again. My brother had barely gotten over his fear that I might die from leukemia. Now he was afraid that having just gone through my health battle, I was not in the right state of mind to make a decision that significantly impacted my life, and his as well.

The rift with Andrew was completely upsetting Mircea's image of who I was and how my life would now unfold. The crisis rocked his sense of family stability—Andrew was a large part of that stability because he balanced both my dad and me. As Laura puts it today, "Both you and your dad are hardheaded, strong-willed people. If one butts heads with Albin, especially, that person will either win or lose. Andrew and Albin were such complete opposites that they had mutual respect for each other and didn't butt heads. This reduced conflict all around."

In other words, Andrew didn't rock the boat. My dad saw him as trustworthy and predictable; my mom, having lived with my dad for decades, saw my husband as mellow, even-tempered, and easy to be around. So what more could I possibly want? You don't just walk away from a marriage where there's no infidelity or abuse. What was my problem? Clearly, I *was* the boat rocker, and an irrational one at that. By impulsively caving in to my own unhappiness, I was spreading needless misery throughout the family. The general sentiment was that I was selfish and ungrateful. As my mother once asked me, "How can you be happy when you're making everyone else *unhappy?*" I didn't have an answer.

Laura could see everyone's perspective better than I could. As she told me recently, "Andrew had been in your life for so long that it was just unimaginable to the rest of the family that he suddenly be cut out. I don't think they saw Andrew and you as husband and wife—you were all just family. Your parents have a very Eastern European way of looking at life, and I don't think they could separate from that and see you, after the cancer, as a woman with a different set of wants and needs."

It was as if I were personally attacking them. I had always been the good girl with the good grades and the right appeasing attitude. Even when I became a professional athlete with a practice-until-you-drop mentality, I still lived close to home and called my parents every day. Now it seemed as if I'd suddenly turned on them, becoming a dark version of my former self, to make their lives a living hell.

In all of our minds, my decision to step back from my marriage was linked to my bout with leukemia, although each of us had our own particular spin on what that meant. At one point in this whole ugly drama, my father actually called my oncologist to ask him if all the chemotherapy could have somehow damaged me psychologically. My parents and brother knew me one way before the cancer and a completely different way afterward. As a doctor, Dad wanted to come up with a medical explanation, hoping they could get the problem fixed and then everything would return to normal. Of course there wasn't a medical explanation—nothing had infected my brain, despite the fact that my family thought I was acting crazy, impulsively throwing my life away by abandoning the one man who truly cared for me.

There was no question that the cancer had changed me, but in my mind, I was finally discovering myself. I was learning about my needs and wants, learning to make decisions for myself, and learning how to stand on my own two feet. Through the trauma of cancer, I became stronger, more introspective, more fixed in my views, and more confident in my own judgment.

MEANWHILE, I STILL HAD TENNIS TO THINK ABOUT. Since coming back from New York in November 2002, my arm had been in a sling while my shoulder slowly healed. I began rehab as soon as I could with a noted tennis-savvy physical therapist named Gary Kitchell whom Justin had recommended. It was only a week or so after the surgery—and right at the beginning of this family battle—when I first made the hour-and-a-half drive up to Vero Beach to meet with "Kitch," as everyone calls him.

I was probably three minutes into the discussion of my shoulder when I totally broke down. Between sobs, I told Kitch that I was having problems in my marriage and my whole family was turning against me. I was supposed to be there to talk about rehabbing my shoulder, and the poor guy was face-to-face with an emotional train wreck. Yet Kitch listened empathetically and just took it all in. It was the beginning of a friendship that grew and deepened throughout this dark passage in my life.

Kitch's home became my temporary sanctuary for the next month. I stayed with him and his family in Vero while rehabbing my shoulder, and he completely distracted me with his quick humor and high spirits. Being around him was the perfect antidote to the tension I inevitably had to return to.

As I said, my impulse was to get away from all that constant pressure and figure things out on my own. But that wasn't going to happen. "You can't just leave a marriage!" my family members all announced, virtually in unison. "You've got to stay and work it out." I could see their point. From their perspective, I'd been madly in love with Andrew, he and I had gotten married, and now there were problems with the marriage, just like there are with many marriages. What I couldn't quite get across to them was something I knew to be true in my heart: that it was hard for me to identify with the love I'd once felt for Andrew. My love for him had been connected to so many other things in the past—dependence, comfort, career—and everyone was trying to get me back to a place I couldn't relate to anymore. I was caught between seeming heartless and hypocritical.

Given the circumstances, I made a good-faith effort to find professional help to sort things out. Andrew and I saw Katia Deac, my cousin's psychiatrist wife, a few times, but always separately.

Meanwhile, my dad had the idea that I should see a local priest who was also trained as a psychologist. It was like getting both religious and psychological counseling at the same time. Initially this priest/shrink saw Andrew and me separately, and unfortunately for the pro-marriage contingency in my family, my dad picked the wrong guy. He didn't adhere to the traditional Catholic married-for-life argument. He saw my side from the very beginning.

In sessions with me alone, the priest was completely forthright, in essence saying, "I completely understand why you want a divorce. You were 15 years old when you got involved with your husband. You were led into something you neither understood nor were prepared to handle. I mean, what does anyone know at 15?"

Along the same lines, at one point Andrew pulled out a letter that I'd written him when I was in fact a love-struck 15-year-old, effusive in my teenage adoration for him. I remember responding to this proof of my undying affection by gently pointing out that I was very young when I wrote that. And his response was, "So?" Which is exactly how my family felt—if I loved him then, why didn't I love him now?

All of this made no sense to me. How could my parents be just fine, even in retrospect, with their 15-year-old daughter getting involved with a 26-year-old man, yet now be so enraged that this same (yet older and wiser) daughter was having doubts?

My dad became as enraged with my priest/counselor as he was with me. He'd thought the good father was going to knock some sense into me, telling me to make the marriage work because no other options were available. The priest went even further in the other direction, saying that he would have no problem annulling my marriage, since the circumstances warranted it. When I confessed to him how guilty I felt about the whole situation, he bluntly replied, "You have nothing to feel guilty about."

Laura was the only family member who thought that all of this professional intervention was a bit of a charade. I certainly didn't. Maybe it seems like a charade in hindsight, but it definitely did not when we were going through it. I didn't want to even think about ending my marriage without thoroughly examining how I was feeling, and why. I simply knew that I felt trapped and suffocated and wanted to know how to deal with it, but I wasn't set on any particular future course at the time.

Later on, Laura expressed the view that "the counseling was more devastating to Andrew than probably anything else. He had a false sense of hope for months." Laura was good friends with Andrew and loved him dearly, and tried to advise him that things might not work out. Andrew chose to hold on to any glimmer of hope. Given his feelings about the marriage, I could hardly blame him—but I wasn't trying to string him along.

ONE NIGHT DURING THIS CRISIS, my dad was on the phone with me, continuing his assault on his selfish, ungrateful daughter. He summed up his frustration in one deadly remark: "You know, your having leukemia was better than this." I was crushed. What he was saying was that he'd rather have me be close to dying than shatter his illusion of family unity. I hung up the phone, crumpled to the ground, and sobbed uncontrollably.

After I peeled myself off the floor that night, I walked outside and called Justin. I hadn't talked to him since we'd parted company in New York right before Thanksgiving. When he picked up the phone, I didn't even say hello. I simply said, "Please tell me something good about myself." I could only see myself at that point through the eyes of my denouncers—as a selfish ingrate and home wrecker. Justin's reaction was: "Something good about you? Are you kidding?" It turns out he had a stack of letters he'd written to me in the last month and hadn't sent. He began to read the beautifully written letters now, one after the other, and they were overflowing with love and kindness. He had an endless stockpile of good things to say about me. When he finished, I thought, *This is the one person on Earth right now who feels this way about me.*

After that call, Justin and I didn't speak again for a while. He'd certainly served as a catalyst in all of this, but ultimately I knew he wasn't the reason for my breakup and I planned on keeping my distance. Nevertheless, it was comforting to have a loving, caring friend when the people closest to me were screaming that I was making the biggest mistake of my life—a mistake that I would regret forever.

Getting therapy didn't change the situation much, so Andrew and I agreed that separating briefly might do us both some good. He decided to visit his parents in Australia over the Christmas holidays, thus leaving me alone with my loving family for two nerve-wracking weeks. We tried hard to be civil, but the whole situation was painfully strained.

On Christmas morning, I went to my parents' house wearing a T-shirt that said Naughty on the back and Promises to Be Nice next Year on the front. They certainly didn't double over in laughter, but I got a perverse kick out of it. We suffered through the Christmas ritual, and then I escaped to my own home, laid on the couch, and watched old movies. Strangely, I wasn't sad or depressed. In the midst of all this madness, I was just grateful to be alone.

When Andrew came back from Australia, we continued counseling for a few more weeks, but I eventually decided that no amount of intervention was going to repair our marriage. If anything, the therapy sessions gave me more emotional clarity and incentive to take the next step. It did nothing, however, to relieve the guilt. The soul-crushing, gut-wrenching guilt.

I finally resolved to tell Andrew that I wanted to end things. I drove home from a rehab session with Kitch, filled with absolute dread at what I was about to do. The weight on my heart and mind was unbearable. I didn't want to see the anguish in Andrew's face or the anger and disappointment in the eyes of my family. I didn't want to be the person ruining someone else's life plan. I knew that I was inciting a new (and perhaps more costly) round of emotional turmoil, but I also knew there was no turning back. This was something I had to do. I finally made it home, and with my heart in my throat, I said it:

"I can't do this anymore. I want a divorce."

Andrew, undoubtedly devastated, shed a few tears, but he was never a person to make a scene. Maybe he knew what was coming; after all, it had been building for months. In some kind of surreal daze, we began going through the house and briefly discussing which things to keep and which to sell. It was a bizarre scenario, but I think we were both just numb from the realization of what was happening.

Shortly after that fateful conversation, I was scheduled to go back to New York for a follow-up visit with my orthopedist. I was away for a few days, and by the time I came back to Boca, Andrew had started the process of packing up the house. However, he was no longer staying there—he had moved in with my parents! Genuinely worried about his emotional well-being and fearing that he could no longer be left alone, my parents had invited Andrew into their home. Needless to say, this was an unsettling turn of events, at least for me. My estranged husband was now living with my increasingly estranged parents.

I kept thinking back to my mom's question: "How can you be happy when you're making everyone else unhappy?" I was not only building a wall between my family and me with this divorce, I was also devastating Andrew. As difficult as it was to stand my ground in the face of all this suffering and discord, I found strength in the belief that I was making the right decision. If I wavered in any way, it would only prolong the inevitable. In spite of the guilt and anguish, I had to keep moving forward.

I was now alone in my home while Andrew and my parents were together, an arrangement that no doubt helped ease the pain of betrayal and abandonment Andrew must have keenly felt. For the last ten years, his life had been completely intertwined with mine. At this juncture, he was the favored child and I was the in-law, the family outsider, the crazy-maker. My dad, as he later admitted, identified with Andrew's emotional collapse and wanted to help—apparently he couldn't see the agony *I* was going through. I think he felt that because the divorce was my decision, I wasn't suffering; or if I was, I had made my bed so now I had to lie in it. The situation was forced on Andrew, and on my family, and my mother and father related to the pain he felt. In a way, it bonded them even more.

My parents also picked up at some point that Justin was in the picture, if only tangentially, and as I could have predicted, they immediately jumped on him as the source of all this strife. "If you leave Andrew for Justin," they told me, "you're making a big, big mistake." I tried to tell them the truth: I wasn't leaving Andrew for Justin. I was just leaving Andrew, period.

Justin had now become the unwitting bogeyman in this drama.

NOT LONG AFTER ANDREW AND I HAD AGREED TO DIVORCE, Kitch left for California to work with Michael Chang, a former French Open champion. I finally had the excuse I was looking for to get away from my family, so I flew out to L.A. to stay with Kim and continue my rehab with Kitch. Andrew and I initiated divorce proceedings, and he prepared to move back to Australia. We worked with one lawyer who was preparing all the materials for the formal filing. The plan was that when I returned from L.A., Andrew would be in Australia, the divorce would be proceeding, and we could both start new lives.

As Andrew was preparing to head Down Under, Justin was just coming back from playing tennis there. Knowing that I was now in the process of getting divorced—and being the aggressive, take-charge guy that he was—he headed for L.A. and came directly to Kim's house from the airport. He wasn't waiting around. This was the opening he had long hoped for, and he was going for it.

As I settled into a routine of working with Kitch and hanging out with Justin, my parents traveled to California for the 2003 Super Bowl. A dinner was planned. They wanted to see me, but I didn't want to face them alone, so Kitch volunteered to come with me as moral support. The situation sounded perfect: Kitch had no involvement in the divorce; and in his unique, engaging way, I hoped he could direct the conversation away from the whole sordid subject.

Well, that strategy didn't take. To this day, it was the most brutal meal I have ever had to sit through. While Kitch was bending over backward to be congenial, my parents were probably at the peak of their anger toward me. It gave them a common cause and probably brought them closer than they'd been in years. This was the one thing they could completely agree on: I was insane.

My 25th birthday had just passed, and at one point in the conversation, Kitch noted that. He then said sweetly, "You know, you have a wonderful daughter." My mother's surly response: "Yeah, she was wonderful for 24 years."

It went on like that for the entire meal. My father in particular would find a way to inject a cutting remark about the divorce into every sentence. We could have been talking about the weather, and my dad would completely go off topic, saying something like, "That's what people do. They quit." And he jumped on any nice thing poor Kitch said.

For someone who had lived her life trying to please her family and keep the peace, this hostility was especially devastating. I couldn't wait for that meal to be over. I sat quietly, took the heat, and simply tried to get through it.

As it turned out, my dad wasn't finished. After dinner, he asked Kitch to wait outside while he took me aside for one more harangue. He had a whole speech prepared. He stared me down and said that he was never going to accept anyone in my life again unless I was married to that person for at least three years, after which Dad might consider inviting him into the family. But if that person happened to be Justin Gimelstob, my father would *never* accept him. He didn't want to have anything to do with Justin. In Hollywood terms, Justin was a deal breaker.

After he finished reading me the riot act, I went to find Kitch to get the hell out of there. Kitch didn't say a word. He just shook his head, gave me a big hug, and finally said, "I am so sorry."

We then went up the road and found a place to have a drink—we both needed an alcoholic beverage or two. Kitch had heard all the stories since we'd begun working together in Vero Beach, but he really couldn't comprehend the level of anger and rejection I was facing until he saw it firsthand. Any relief I was feeling that the divorce was over and I could resume my life was completely shattered by that dinner.

That wasn't the end of the attacks, though. Soon after, tucked in with some investment information my dad had left with my lawyer, he included a nasty letter. For three pages he went on, issuing a litany of ultimatums, including his three-year rule, which would apply to anyone except Justin. In addition, he'd decided that he would never watch me play tennis again. He had enjoyed it for the first 19 years, but no more. In effect, he was now washing his hands of the very thing he'd forced me to do in the first place!

Although Andrew and I only had one lawyer between us and everything seemed pretty amicable, there was one point of dispute about the distribution of a certain financial fund. I'm not sure Andrew was even part of the dispute, but my father certainly was. On Andrew's behalf, Dad called our lawyer and said that Andrew should be getting a bigger cut. When I heard about this from the lawyer, I stood my ground, insisting that the arrangement remain as I'd requested. What did my dad have to do with this anyway?

Afterward, I called him and tightly said, "I know you disapprove of this whole divorce, but I would appreciate it if you would stay out of our finances." He went nuts, telling me something to the effect that if this was the way I felt, fine, but he was willing to hire another lawyer for Andrew and fight me for more of my money. I was about to enter into a court battle with my own father!

That never happened, but something in me snapped during that little chat. The extremes my parents had gone to through this whole episode were mind-boggling to me, but this was the capper. Each scathing word and each hurtful comment cut me to the core. Family or not, I had to step away. Right after that call to my dad, I remember thinking, *That's it. From this point forward, I have to detach myself. I can't let them hurt me anymore, and I can't look for their approval in everything I do. It's not my responsibility to make them happy. I have to live my life the way I want.*

DURING THIS TUMULTUOUS PERIOD, I was named the WTA Comeback Player of the Year. This honor, along with the Player of the Year and other WTA awards, is voted on by the global tennis media. Lindsay and Chanda Rubin had also been nominated for the award, both coming back after injuries, and both with much better win-loss records for the year than I had. Justin, who was in Miami when I accepted the award, had a take on it that bordered on inappropriate. But, as was often the case, I found what he said hilarious because it struck me as quite accurate. He jokingly dubbed it the "Thanks for Not Dying" Award.

The award was a welcome, if momentary, sign that I'd done something positive and commendable. Yet I was still in the aftermath of the divorce, guilt-ridden, fighting with my family, and in general feeling like crap about myself. I wasn't in quite the right frame of mind to fully appreciate it.

Luckily, just a few months later, my shoulder was healing, thanks to many hours with Kitch. I stayed in my Florida home and started practicing in earnest. Lindsay got married in Hawaii in April, so I flew out for that grand occasion. I didn't see Justin much, though. I was trying to process my divorce and take things slowly with him, and I succeeded for a short while . . . although that wasn't easy to do, given his trademark persistent manner, not to mention my own need to feel loved and wanted after the divorce and the estrangement from my family.

I finally got back to Tour play in Strasbourg, France, a lead-up tournament to the French Open. I won my first round, beating Iveta Benesova, then lost to Anastasia Myskina. At the French a week later, I played Daja Bedanova in the first round and won my first Grand Slam singles match since the cancer. After the drama and turmoil of the previous two years, it was a sweet victory. And I felt as if I'd done it on my own. I wasn't happy without the support of my family, but I *was* dealing with it. I was also winning despite my personal circumstances, and that gave me a much-needed sense of pride and independence.

At that point I was again hampered by injury. In Birmingham, England, at one of the lead-up tournaments to Wimbledon, I developed an irritation on the undersurface of my right kneecap, which was incredibly uncomfortable. I played Wimbledon in significant pain and lost in the first round. Then I teamed with Rennae Stubbs in doubles, and we played Serena and Venus in our first match and lost in three sets. Because of my knee, I had to withdraw from the rest of 2003's summer tournaments. I didn't get back on the court until the U.S. Open in late August.

Back home, I put the exclamation point on my vow to live my own life by selling the house in Florida and moving to Newport Beach, California. I had my support team, Kim and Lindsay, ready to smooth this transition. In fact, I moved to Orange County mainly because Lindsay was there. Up to that point we had been good friends; after my move, we became like sisters. Lindsay was wonderfully supportive not only emotionally but also logistically—she showed me where to look for apartments, where to buy groceries, where to get my hair cut. Most important, she was someone I could lean on for support and encouragement during one of the toughest periods of my life. Lindsay truly helped me through the opening stages of my new incarnation.

While I was slowly putting the pieces of my personal life back together, getting my career back on track was another story. I had one physical problem after another: My knee healed, and I played the U.S. Open; I lost in the first round, and my shoulder flared up again. Unfortunately, my surgery had not succeeded in alleviating my pain. In the back of my mind, I knew that the only way to proceed was to have a second surgery and then go through those months of recovery and rehab all over again. I wasn't sure at that point if I had it in me to survive that ordeal a second time.

I had come to another fork in the road. When I started my comeback after the leukemia, I was playing with a renewed passion for the game. I'd clearly worked my way back to a high level of play, but constant injuries were undermining my progress. I wasn't getting the results I had hoped for, and my passion was waning. The frustration was palpable. Maybe the injuries were telling me something. Maybe I had gone as far as I could in my comeback. Maybe it was time to hang it up for good.

When I first returned to playing after the cancer, it was thrilling. I was enamored by both the physical challenge and the enormous outpouring of support and encouragement I was getting from the tennis world. But that was in July 2002. By the fall of 2003, no one remembered that I'd had leukemia, "beat" it, and made it back to the Tour. By this time, I was just another player in the draw. No one was coming up after a match and saying, "Hey, great job of getting back!" I didn't need constant validation, but all that enthusiasm did add to the excitement of being out there, an excitement that I clearly wasn't feeling anymore.

I appreciated my comeback, but tennis suddenly felt insignificant. As a professional player, the game is an all-important, all-consuming activity, demanding that one be completely egocentric and focused on winning. In my circumstance, having left the sport completely and then returning with a whole new mind-set about my life, I had one foot in both worlds—the tennis world and the real world. It only took a series of bad breaks to burst the bubble of self-absorption demanded by my chosen profession. After being forced to pull out of a tournament in Beijing because of my injured shoulder, I remember asking myself, "What am I doing? Is this really that important? Is this what I should be doing now?"

I had more or less convinced myself that I was ready to retire when Justin and I went on a vacation to Hawaii in November with Lindsay and her new husband, Jon. I told Lindsay about my current attitude toward tennis, and she had an idea: maybe I should stop playing singles altogether and concentrate entirely on doubles. And she would be my doubles partner again. She didn't want to play doubles full-time, since she was still one of the best singles players in the world. But she still wanted to play *some* doubles—and the idea was that we could travel together, the strain on my shoulder would be reduced, and tennis would become more fun and less of a chore for me.

It was a gracious offer, but I was hesitant to make yet another commitment in the face of my injuries and my disenchantment with the game. Justin encouraged me to say yes. "You have to do it," he said, in his uniquely insistent way. "It's a great opportunity." I finally agreed. I'd give tennis—at least doubles play, anyway—one last shot.

I didn't go home for Thanksgiving that year, or even for Christmas, which was a first for me. A full year after I'd announced my unhappiness with my marriage, my mother had come around, but my relationship with my father was still strained. And although my brother might have still been irked by the divorce, he was never outwardly angry or uncivil. So instead of Boca, I went to Park City, Utah, for Christmas to be with Mircea, Laura, Collin, and Laura's family. Ironically, I felt more comfortable with my sister-in-law's family than my own.

THE 2004 TENNIS SEASON BEGAN, AS ALWAYS, with the lead-up tournaments to the Australian Open. Now that I was only playing doubles, there was much less strain on my shoulder. I was still in pain but could play through it. Lindsay and I reached the semifinals in Sydney and defeated top-seeded Martina Navratilova and Lisa Raymond en route. I enjoyed playing with my good friend again after almost three years.

After Sydney, Lindsay and I moved on to the Australian Open in Melbourne. In the second round, Lindsay and I beat Martina Navratilova and Lisa Raymond for the second straight time. Unfortunately, Lindsay and I couldn't maintain the momentum and lost our third-round match the next day.

Lindsay and I then made an unspectacular showing at the next tournament in Tokyo. Yet my father contacted me there to say that he and my mother were headed to L.A. for a medical meeting. He offered to pick me up at the airport when I came in. This was a shock. After a year of barely speaking, it was surprising that he wanted to greet me at the airport and take me to my new home, a symbol of my newfound independence.

When I spotted my parents outside the baggage-claim area at LAX, my father gave me a huge bear hug, and instantly I knew that everything had changed. My mom's period of alienation had been relatively brief, but my dad had shown no signs up to that moment of forgiving me for what he saw as impulsive, irresponsible behavior. I now realized that I had been accepted back into the fold.

This may seem odd, but I didn't feel the need to dredge up any of the past with my parents. I was just happy to have my family back. On some level, I understood that the estrangement from my dad was temporary. I always knew deep down that he would never completely turn his back on me. He'd been hurt by the divorce, and his behavior toward me was a reaction to his own pain. His hurt manifested itself as anger, his temper flared, and he said things he didn't mean. I got that, forgave him, and accepted him back, just as he finally accepted me back after the pain he perceived I had caused him. Our family bond was strong, and although it may have been severely bent, I always knew it had never truly been broken.

My parents and I had a wonderful time together, never really talking about what had transpired. I showed them my place in Newport Beach, and in his loving and generous way of trying to spoil everyone around him, Dad took Mom and me to the upscale Fashion Island shopping mall and bought me a watch for my birthday, which had just passed. That was it—after a pleasant afternoon together, almost a year and a half of recrimination and terribly hurt feelings just disappeared. It was another year or more before my father felt comfortable enough to address some of the awful things he had said in the heat of the divorce, but as of that day in Southern California, all was right in my family, if not the world.

• • •   • • •

Chapter 8

THE PHOENIX

I was back in the good graces of my family, but my relationship with Justin was taking a toll on me. It was a volatile and passionate affair from the very beginning, and trying to keep things on an even keel exacted a high price. Our relationship was like a roller coaster, filled with ecstatic highs and soul-crushing lows. We were both trying to pursue our individual careers, and Justin's behavior was often affected by the outcome of his tennis matches. My almost desperate desire to use our relationship to escape the pain of my illness, divorce, and family problems only compounded the drama. Instead of really examining all the underlying problems in my life, I constantly ran from my inner demons, replacing one set of issues with another.

And my relationship wasn't my only escape. After my illness, I became more conscious of my eating habits, what I put into my body, and how it made me feel. I also changed my workouts and got in the best shape of my life. Working out was another way for me to feel alive again, and since it was part of my job, I had every excuse to overdo it. It made me feel good and it was healthy, so naturally I thought I'd play better. But it quickly became an unhealthy obsession.

As my personal and professional life started to unravel, maniacal conditioning gave me a sense of control in the midst of the chaos. I would run four miles every morning, often before doubles matches. There were times I would run in the morning, practice or play a match, and then go back to the gym for more punishment. I'd go through periods of sadness and depression where I barely ate. I was running—literally—from my internal pain.

Despite my fanatical fitness, my physical problems on the tennis court only got worse. I finally made the decision to have a second surgery on my shoulder in May, which meant that my return to all-doubles play with Lindsay as my partner would now have to be put on hold.

I flew to New York once again for the procedure, and my orthopedist and I finally figured out what was wrong with my shoulder. The first diagnosis had been inaccurate, which explained Dr. Altchek's puzzlement after the first surgery. I had what is known as a coracoid impingement, a rare and painful disorder. After the procedure to ameliorate this condition, my shoulder definitely improved. But, as I found out going forward, my arm was significantly weakened by the two surgeries. My shoulder never came close to feeling as strong as it did before I got cancer. I played the rest of my career with varying degrees of inflammation, stiffness, soreness, and pain.

After the surgery, I returned to California to rehab. The next four or five months are a blur to me now, a lost period of exercise and training, as well as traveling with Justin as he continued on the Tour. Not surprisingly, my boyfriend was extremely emotional about his tennis. He played with incredible intensity, but he also had the tendency to take his on-court frustrations out on the people closest to him. And I was the person closest to him at that time.

It is actually not all that uncommon for tennis players to take their on-court frustrations out on their coach, spouse, or others on the sidelines. Something about the extremely personal nature of one-on-one competition often generates intense emotion that some professional athletes have a difficult time managing. Throughout my tennis life, I had seen many examples of this misdirected anger. I'd learned about anger and tennis early on. In fact, when Justin got mad at me while he was losing or after he lost a match, it was reminiscent of my dad getting mad at me after *I* lost a match. In both situations, it stung deeply and I felt completely helpless. As a child, I didn't have the option of walking away, and I'd obviously carried those feelings of powerlessness with me as an adult. Aside from voicing my dismay, I really never did anything about what I viewed as inappropriate behavior. I was used to being hurt directly or indirectly by tennis—or by the way people closest to me *reacted* to tennis—so I accepted it and continued to find it difficult to walk away.

Justin would inevitably apologize for his outbursts, but his focus would quickly return to himself and his game. As I said, playing pro tennis demands a certain level of selfishness, so in a way I understood that Justin needed to do certain things for himself and his career, but going to tournaments and *not* playing was tough on me. My career was clearly wobbling, if not waning, and I couldn't find my place at tournaments when I wasn't playing. I was in a familiar environment in an oddly unfamiliar capacity. There were often times when I needed support and a sympathetic ear, and he was simply not in a place to listen to my woes.

I was constantly conflicted. I stayed with Justin and tried to be supportive, understanding, and forgiving; but I felt confused and unsure of myself, struggling in the aftermath of the cancer, my divorce, and my shoulder surgeries. Justin gave me a sense of stability, and I was clinging to him for dear life, hoping he'd make me feel loved, safe, and whole. Our relationship was all I felt I had at that point. Without tennis, I began to attach my self-esteem to the success of my relationship instead of the success of my career, and that no doubt added to the pressure and expectations Justin felt I was placing on him.

It was probably a relief for him when I went back to Florida to be with my family. Ironically, after the dust had settled with my parents, Florida had become my new sanctuary. With the birth of my second nephew, Chet, on July 15, 2004, I felt even more drawn there. My nephews were (and still are) the loves of my life. Their innocence and unconditional love always manage to lift my spirits—so much so that when I was having a difficult time on the road, Raj would ask me to get to a place where I felt nothing but happiness. My "happy place," as he'd jokingly call it, was with my nephews. Simply thinking of them always made me feel better.

I FINALLY STARTED PLAYING AGAIN AT THE U.S. OPEN in late August but remember little about it. I also tried to resurrect my singles career by playing in a couple of small tournaments, but my heart wasn't in it. My chronically aching shoulder couldn't handle the stress, and my mind couldn't handle the thought of yet another comeback. I was exhausted and felt completely defeated.

The entire period was, in retrospect, an absolute debacle.

The person I counted on through all periods, good and bad, was Raj. He was much more than a tennis coach. Since we'd begun working together in 2002, he'd become my mentor, friend, and counselor. Besides helping me tremendously to adapt my play to get the best I could out of my post-cancer body, Raj was the person I turned to when I was frustrated with my career, family, or relationship. Over the course of those three years, I must have shown up crying on the court at least once a week. Like my preteen heart-to-heart talks with Tim Gullikson, Raj spent half his time coaching me and the other half helping me work through my numerous issues.

Starting the year fresh after the disaster of 2004, he and I arrived in Auckland, New Zealand, in early 2005 so that I could play a warm-up tournament to the Australian Open. Lindsay wasn't available for that week, so I played doubles with Jill Craybas, another player who worked with Raj. We played our first round at night and it was extremely cold and windy, which was always tough on my shoulder. I was uncomfortable, my shoulder was stiff, and I was serving one double fault after another. I didn't have any feeling, strength, or confidence in my shoulder, or my play. Jill and I ended up losing to two unknown players, 6-4, in the third set.

The next day when I showed up to practice with Raj, I was as foul as foul could be. I was moping around, slamming balls into the fence for no reason, just generally pissed off at the world. Most of my close friends in tennis, with the notable exception of Lindsay, had retired by then. I felt completely alone, angry, and disappointed . . . and I had no desire to hide it.

Five minutes into practice, Raj stopped, turned to me, and asked, "Okay, what's going on with you?" I unloaded, bitching about anything and everything. I told him that I was absolutely miserable, was playing like crap, had lost all my confidence, and hated all things associated with tennis. I hated walking into the players' lounge, I said, because I had no desire to see anyone. None of the women were really my friends—they were all these pro tennis players who were sheltered, pampered, narcissistic, and insulated in this unreal "bubble world" that had nothing to do with real life (never mind that I was one of those players myself). The rant continued for quite a while. I had completely lost my mind.

Raj finally replied, "Okay, I get it. But you might want to think about what *you* are putting into this equation." He always had a way of calling me out and telling me the truth in a way that was rarely combative or belittling. And however reluctantly, I listened. He went on to explain that "people often respond to you in the way you are behaving toward them, and whole situations can unfold according to the way you view them going in." He then ended his little talk by saying that he thought I was too emotional at that point to discuss the matter further. He wanted me to leave the practice, go back to my hotel room, and spend the day writing down exactly what I was feeling.

In a huff, I grudgingly agreed to do what he asked and retired to my room, still full of rage. I sat down to write my thoughts, knocked out all of three sentences, and abandoned my assignment. "This is ridiculous," I told myself. "I know exactly how I'm feeling. I'm *pissed!*"

A couple of hours later, having calmed down a little, I decided to have another go at it. And suddenly, my emotions came out like a flash flood. I started writing and crying and crying and writing, and the three sentences turned into three single-spaced pages of how, at age 26, I felt like a failure. In the short span of three years, I'd gone from feeling extremely proud that I'd survived leukemia and returned to professional tennis, to the emotional state I was in now—demoralized, embittered, and almost ashamed that I was "just" a doubles player. I had completely bought into the attitude that an accomplished doubles player is somehow a lesser human being than an accomplished singles player. And I was even failing at that! I was humiliated and embarrassed.

On top of everything, I selfishly missed having Andrew around as a person totally dedicated to my well-being. Justin was absorbed in his own career, and even Raj, as supportive as he was, split his time between Jill Craybas and me. No one was singularly focused on me and my needs. I felt all alone, inadequate, a loser.

I don't think I'd fully realized until that episode how much I'd attached my sense of self-worth to tennis, and probably had since age six. I always saw myself as a well-rounded person capable of having a rich life outside of tennis. But all parts of my life, even after my divorce from Andrew, remained completely entwined with this frustrating career. Who was my boyfriend after my tennis player/coach/husband, Andrew? Another tennis player. And what did I keep coming back to after every injury? Tennis. I might not have been fully content in the tennis world after my leukemia, but it was comfortable, and I was scared to go outside of it. It was the only reality I had ever known.

Raj came to my room that night around ten, and I read him everything I'd written. He was, as always, incredibly supportive. He knew that I was in the middle of an important emotional shift, and he had the foresight not to rush it, not to push me just to get to a conclusion. He left me alone for a couple days after that so I could cry out more of the pain and frustration of the last three years. I slowly came to terms with my situation, which was: I used to be able to serve with authority, but no longer. I used to be able to play singles with authority, but no longer. *It was clearly time to let go of what I used to be capable of and make the best of what I could do now.* This was Raj's gentle advice as I mourned the loss of those skills, and it was advice that finally sank in.

Raj himself put it slightly differently. "One of your real strengths," he later told me, "is that you can actually look with an objective eye at what's being said to you *about* you. When someone holds a mirror up to anyone, they rarely like what they see. You may not like it, but you will process it, take it in, and move away from that place. And that's what happened in Auckland."

Whatever happened in Auckland, it was genuinely cathartic for me. Lindsay was now back as my partner, and although we lost in the first round of the very next tournament in Sydney, I was feeling much better about myself and playing better as a result. I had been relieved, at least temporarily, of my feelings of inadequacy.

LINDSAY AND I MOVED ON TO THE AUSTRALIAN OPEN. My friend had ended 2004 ranked #1 in singles, and this was the first Grand Slam of 2005. The same stress I always felt during tournaments was weighing on her, and it was evident in her behavior. We won our first couple of rounds, but she was on edge, and our practices were filled with tension. I understood what she was going through, but I couldn't control it. What I *could* control, to use Raj's phrase, was what I was putting into the equation. So I focused on myself, my play, and what I could do with what I'd now been given.

Lindsay and I kept winning and found ourselves in the semis. On the same day, she'd just won an exhausting three-hour quarterfinal match in singles. It was a blisteringly hot summer day, and many people—including her husband and her coach—wanted her to pull out of our match. I told her that I'd understand if she wanted to bow out, but she refused. I knew that I was probably the only person she would have taken the court for that day, and while I was incredibly grateful, I also felt more pressure. We were already heavily favored going into the match, and I wanted to play well and finish the match quickly for her because she'd taken the court for me.

I was nervous; she was tired and cranky; and as a team, we were totally out of sync. We started poorly and lost the first set, but we finally found our rhythm and started playing in unison. We won the match, 6-3, in the third. I was happy to be in the final of a Grand Slam for the first time since the cancer—but honestly, I was relieved more than anything else.

I didn't see Lindsay again that day, but when I got back to my room in her suite that night, I found a little present with a note that said: "Here we are again in the finals. We will enjoy."

We had the next day off, and on that Friday, we lost in the finals to Australian Alicia Molik and Russian Svetlana Kuznetsova. Despite the outcome, I felt as victorious as I would have if we'd actually won. In a very emotional speech during the trophy ceremony, I spoke from the heart. "Four years ago," I told the crowd, "I didn't know if I would live, let alone live to play well enough to see another Grand Slam final." I was crying, and Lindsay was crying. When Alicia got up to give her speech, she jokingly mentioned that maybe Kleenex should sign on as a sponsor next year. Coming only two weeks after my breakdown in Auckland, it was easily the most thrilling and satisfying moment in my entire post-cancer career.

Raj also saw it as a moral and psychological victory. As he remembers today: "I thought it was pretty profound that you had the perspective to realize that even in losing, you'd won. The final score in no way defined you. You'd gotten back to the highest level of the game. You didn't have all the tools you had before, but you still had what it took to make it to a Grand Slam final. And Lindsay was very emotional, too. From checking in daily to see how you were doing in the hospital in Miami to standing next to you in Melbourne Park after those years—it was obviously pretty special for both of you."

I was clearly on a mini-roll after Melbourne. I felt that 2005 was shaping up to be my best year, at least in tennis, since 2000. In the next big tournament after the Australian Open, in Tokyo, Lindsay and I made the finals again but also lost again. Then right after that, I got a call from Zina Garrison, the Fed Cup captain, asking me to join the team—along with Lindsay, and Serena and Venus Williams. I was beyond excited, as I recalled that the first time I had been asked to be on the Fed Cup team was still one of the happiest moments of my tennis life.

I vividly remember the day in 1998 when I got that call from Billie Jean King, who was the Fed Cup captain at the time, and how proud I felt to be chosen to represent my country in tennis competition. Being coached by Billie Jean and playing alongside Monica Seles, Lisa Raymond, and Mary Joe Fernandez had been a wonderful experience. This time around, we were scheduled to play in Delray Beach, Florida, all of two miles from where I grew up. I was going back to South Florida to play in front of my hometown crowd!

Personally, things went from bad to worse. After almost two turbulent years together, and one meltdown after another, Justin and I finally agreed to split.

I was genuinely heartbroken. It seemed like yet another failure piled on top of all the others. But, ironically, at that point my tennis was going well, and I was surrounded by people who truly appreciated me. I surprised even myself by snapping out of my sadness and despair relatively quickly. In fact, for the first time in a long time, I realized that I was feeling good about my life. My career was on the upswing, my family and I were getting along, and I was liberated from the drama and tension in my personal life.

After playing a couple of small tournaments, I headed to Florida. The great thing about Fed Cup is that the team practices together the entire week. I was once again in my element—surrounded by a congenial and supportive group, working hard and completely enjoying myself at the same time.

I played well in the doubles, the last of the scheduled matches, even though it was a "dead rubber," meaning that the score didn't count because our American team had already won the competition by virtue of winning the singles matches. Nevertheless, it was a meaningful victory. My entire family came to see me, including my eldest nephew, Collin, who was then four.

Growing up, I'd played many times at the very tennis club in Delray Beach where the competition was held; after everything I'd been through, being there was like coming full circle. Whatever alienation I felt toward Florida—or my family—during those tough years after the divorce, was completely gone. I was the happiest I'd been in years.

RIGHT BEFORE THE FED CUP, I SAT DOWN WITH RAJ to map out my future schedule. Since Lindsay didn't want to play doubles at the next Grand Slam, the French Open, I decided to ask a very accomplished Swiss player named Patty Schnyder to partner with me. I didn't know her very well (she was on the shy side), but I had always liked her and admired her tennis. She was a top-20 singles player for much of her career, and I thought we would match up nicely. There was only one caveat: I told Raj that I didn't want to go to Europe to play a grueling schedule of lead-up tournaments to the French, something I always felt obligated to do.

He looked at me and simply said, "Don't."

I'd clearly been playing on my own terms for a while, but this was still a lightbulb moment for me. Raj was right—I could play whenever and wherever I wanted. I didn't have to do anything I didn't want to do. I asked Patty if she wanted to play the French under these terms, and she said that was fine. The fact that she was so laid-back about it only confirmed that I'd made the right choice.

Since I had a few weeks before the French, I went back to Southern California to practice and just enjoy myself. But if I thought that the Justin situation was settled, I was wrong. He wasn't ready to let things die; and he often had romantic, and sometimes dramatic, ways of reappearing in my life. One night I heard a loud knock at my door . . . and there was Justin, disheveled but full of ardor, wanting to get back together and urging me not to give up on our relationship. He had abruptly hopped on a plane after a tournament in Tunica, Mississippi, flown out to LAX, and driven to my place in Newport Beach, all in one day.

I must admit that his impulsive mission was not entirely in vain. I was extremely hesitant to fall back into a trap that I'd just escaped, but I felt powerless against our crazy love. And that's what it was—a crazy, obsessive, and not necessarily healthy love affair, which the French call "l'amour fou."

We slowly started spending time together after that night, but the French Open allowed me to get some space away from him and get back to tennis. In years past, I'd be exhausted by the time I arrived in Paris. I'd play all the lead-up tournaments, live in hotel rooms for weeks, and just want to go home. This year was different: I arrived in Paris fresh and full of enthusiasm. I hadn't played for the previous five weeks and was thoroughly rested and eager to compete. I decided to live it up a little by splurging on a nice hotel—the Prince de Galles— getting a room right down the hall from Lindsay. I'd never been so relaxed or so happy going into a Grand Slam.

Raj saw this right away. He could tell by the big smile on my face that I was thrilled to be there. In fact, I told him, I was so excited that I really didn't care how well I might do. I was basically telling Raj what he'd been trying to get through my head since we had first started working together four years earlier: If I could release the attachment to the result when I played, I'd play better. I'd enjoy the process and not put as much pressure on myself. I wouldn't fret over every little mistake or overthink the game. That's where I was now, and it was a powerful place.

My dad—the same guy who at one point told me that he never wanted to watch me play again—came to Paris to support me. He'd always loved the French Open and had been coming before I even turned pro. In his typical generous fashion, he took Lindsay and me out to eat at some of the nicest restaurants in town. He and I also spent a lot of time alone. Having coffee one day on the Champs-Élysées, I began to talk to him more freely about my life than I ever had before. We spoke a little about the divorce, and I told him about my current ups and downs with Justin. He was both sympathetic and nonjudgmental. He had come to accept Justin as someone who was in my life.

My dad now seemed to respect me as my own person. At one point in the conversation, he looked at me and said, "You know, I sometimes say things I don't mean, but I usually come around." It was a watershed moment. It was his way of apologizing for all of the unpleasant things said in anger and frustration during that terrible year of the divorce, and maybe over the course of my life. In this simple, honest exchange, I felt closer to him than ever before.

PATTY SCHNYDER AND I HIT IT OFF INSTANTLY, as both partners and players. We had a great time playing together, and there were many moments of laughter on the court. We struggled through our first round mainly because we had never played together, but I felt like I was playing with a tremendous amount of freedom and joy. At one point in our third-round match, I completely misjudged a return on a break point and let the ball go right by me, thinking it was going out. It landed six feet inside the baseline. Patty and I just looked at each other and burst out laughing.

We made it to the quarterfinals and were up against two of the best doubles players in the world, Lisa Raymond and Rennae Stubbs. Having been chosen for that year's Fed Cup over Lisa, I felt I had something to prove, and I took the court on a mission. It was the perfect blend of nerves and excitement, much like I felt when playing Team Tennis at the start of my comeback. I completely went into the zone and played one of the best matches of my career. Patty and I won 6-3, 6-4.

We played our semifinal match on Court Suzanne Lenglen, and because it had rained the night before, the court surface was significantly slower. I could never quite get my timing right. I'd apologize to Patty after hitting a ball into the net, and she'd laugh and say, "That's all right—just try hitting it *over* the net next time." We lost the match, but my new attitude and my new partner took the sting out of losing and doubled the pure pleasure of playing.

Afterward, I again retreated to Florida. While there, I spent a lot of time listening to the powerful autobiographical music of Ani DiFranco. Raj had introduced me to her work around the time I was breaking up with Justin because he thought I would relate to her lyrics. He was right. In one of her songs, "32 Flavors," there's a great line about a phoenix rising up from the ashes that became imprinted in my brain. That image of that ascending phoenix stayed with me. I'd always wanted a tattoo, but one with meaning—now I knew exactly what that tattoo was going to be.

I did some research online, and by the time I got back to L.A., I'd found the design I wanted. The very day I found it, I went to have it embedded in my skin. I decided on the perfect place for my phoenix: on my right back hip where they'd repeatedly extracted my bone marrow during the leukemia treatment.

The first place I tried couldn't fit me in, and I was in no mood to make an appointment. My friend Kim's husband, Oliver, directed me to a parlor in San Pedro where the tattoo artist also told me that she was too busy to take me right away. I was so adamant that she finally relented and tattooed the design in 15 minutes. It was a feeling of empowerment having that phoenix tattooed on the very spot where I'd once felt the least empowered. It symbolized my new attitude toward life: I had a newfound strength, perspective, and appreciation for it. After four long, difficult years, I felt that I was finally coming to terms with the fallout from my illness—the divorce, my family troubles, my compromised career, my relationship with Justin. Or at least I *thought* I was making sense of it all.

LINDSAY AND I JOINED FORCES AGAIN AT WIMBLEDON but lost in the second round. Justin was also there and he played very well, finally losing in the third round to Lleyton Hewitt. Off the court, especially toward me, he was gracious, thoughtful, attentive and, as usual, extremely generous. I stayed in a house with Lindsay, and he was a frequent guest. He ended up staying an extra week to spend time with me as I waited for Lindsay to finish her singles competition so we could go to Moscow together for Fed Cup play. (She eventually lost to Venus

Williams in what ended up being the longest Wimbledon women's singles final ever.)

Unfortunately, the whiplash nature of our relationship soon returned. When I got to the U.S. Open, I stayed with and spent most of my free time with Mircea, by prior arrangement. My brother and I had a great time together, and we were reminded of the old days when he used to travel the world with me. Justin was playing as well, and when he lost, he abruptly left town. I accepted it as par for the course and concentrated on myself, my time with my brother, and my tennis. I played with Patty Schnyder again, and we made it to the quarterfinals at the Open. I also made it to the semifinals in mixed doubles with Mike Bryan.

Then, in a complete about-face, Justin flew back into town and wrote an entire blog dedicated to me for the *Sports Illustrated* Website. An excellent writer, he had been hired by the site to write a series of reports giving an insider's perspective on the Open.

This particular column by, as they described him, "outspoken tennis pro Justin Gimelstob," was entitled "There Goes My Hero," with the subheading, "Morariu beat cancer and injury to do what she loves." It was a public love letter posing as a sports column.

He opened the column like this:

> This year's U.S. Open has an entire menu of feel-good stories. James Blake battling back from injury and his father's death. Andre Agassi spitting in the face of age. Sania Mirza gripping her native India. But there's another one flying underneath the radar who's near and dear to my heart: my own girlfriend.
>
> If you're lucky enough to be at the USTA National Tennis Center on Tuesday, check out Court 11, where Corina Morariu will be competing alongside Patty Schnyder in the women's doubles quarterfinals. Or stop by the Grandstand later to see Morariu in the quarters of mixed doubles, where she's partnering with Mike Bryan.
>
> Corina is an incredible person, and the story of her past four-and-a-half years is inspiring. In 2001, at age 23, Corina was diagnosed with acute promyelocytic leukemia. For a while, the prognosis was very poor. But with the aid of brilliant, loving doctors and nurses, she was able to endure the harsh chemotherapy treatment needed for recovery.

Her return to health is a testament to her unwavering resolve and will to live. But that only tells half of the story, the half of things that she couldn't control.

He then went on to talk about my victories at Wimbledon and elsewhere and how, after the cancer, I had played "a memorable match against Serena Williams on opening night of the '02 Open, and the whole world saw what a true comeback looked like."

Then he mentioned my many shoulder problems and ended the column like this:

Corina remained undeterred. While the latest shoulder surgery has shelved her singles career, she has had great success in doubles this year, reaching the finals of the Australian Open and the Toray Pan Pacific Open in Tokyo, the semifinals of the French Open and, once again, representing her country in Fed Cup play.

This past July at Wimbledon, Corina passed the monumental three-year mark of being cancer-free. Her determination and grace through adversity has been remarkable—it's a lesson everyone could learn from.

Make sure you watch this beautiful woman play tennis, and see for yourself what a hero looks like. I'll be in the front row, cheering the loudest.

I was moved by this public display of affection. It was the nicest thing anyone had ever written about me—and Justin's most forceful public declaration of love.

PATTY AND I CONTINUED TO PLAY TOGETHER for a series of tournaments in Europe and then, after the last one, she told me that she'd decided not to play doubles the next year. This came as a genuine shock to me. By this point, my other all-time favorite partner, Lindsay, had also decided to stop playing doubles. I felt I was out of options.

I loved playing with Patty, and we got along so well that I couldn't imagine finding someone to replace her. I remember standing in a hallway in Zurich, telling Raj, "I think my career is over." I just didn't see where to go from there. I thought it might be a step in the wrong direction to play with anyone other than Patty or Lindsay. Raj's advice was that I should go home, relax, and think about it. We'd make that decision later.

Meanwhile, after several more arguments in the fall, Justin and I reconciled once again and were back to planning our future together. He'd previously purchased a house in Santa Monica and was living there full-time, so we were spending a lot of time in that home and enjoying it. The lease on my apartment in Orange County was up at the end of the year, so I decided to move in with him when my lease expired.

I'm sure this decision baffled others in my life. The rapid-fire, back-and-forth nature of this "amour fou" was too confusing for even me to follow—the fighting, the making up, the breaking up, the getting back together. It was a tumultuous and vicious cycle, and I often felt like I was in emotional agony. My whole affair with Justin was like a drug: I was completely addicted, riding this roller coaster of emotional highs and lows—loving the highs, feeling wretched during the lows. The more I kept coming back, the worse I felt about myself—like a junkie who felt intense self-loathing while in the very act of shooting up. I started to dislike the person I was in the relationship: desperate, conflicted, and unsure.

Consciously or not, I needed the chaos. Initially, it was an exciting change of pace from the predictable rhythm of my marriage to Andrew. And in the wake of the leukemia, the intense feelings, good and bad, made me feel alive after I had been so close to death. They were like a fire—they lit me up and burned me at the same time. Being with Justin was excitement with a heavy price tag, and when it wore me down to the point that I was ready to stop, I couldn't. No matter how much I despised the chaos, I was habituated to it. I had been dealing with chaos my entire life, and I knew how to function in the dysfunction. It was familiar—damaging to my mental health, for sure, but familiar.

What made me successful as an athlete (and what helped me in my battle with leukemia) was the attitude I brought to my personal life. As a player, I was used to enduring a certain amount of physical and emotional pain to achieve an eventual goal. I didn't give up. I could endure arduous training sessions and heartbreaking losses with the knowledge that the hard work and emotional agony would one day pay off. I applied the same mind-set to my relationship: I knew the kind of relationship I wanted and would even see occasional glimpses of it, but there was always something I just had to "get through" standing in the way.

What I didn't realize was that with each scathing word and debilitating argument, I wasn't getting closer to my "goal" of sustaining a healthy relationship. Instead, the foundation of my relationship was continually cracking. It was agonizing, but I was committed to making it work, no matter how miserable I often was in the process.

I moved my stuff into Justin's house, and we tried to forget all the difficult times together and just focus on the good ones, like the two weeks at Wimbledon. Now a new tennis season was on the horizon, and I was stuck. After a rough emotional start, 2005 had been a great year tenniswise. I'd made it back to a Grand Slam final, made the Fed Cup team, and had in general proven to the tennis world (and myself) that I'd staged a full-fledged comeback.

I could quit now with my head held high, but I was still hesitant to do so. The last time I felt this way, it was Lindsay who had talked me out of it. This time it was Justin. He thought that traveling to tournaments and playing alongside each other would give us the opportunity to spend more time together.

It sounded like a good idea at the time.

• • • • • •

Chapter 9

ONE LAST GO

Justin and I moved in together during the off-season, which was a perfect time to settle into our new living arrangement. I really loved our neighborhood in Santa Monica, and we both saw the house as a place where we could be happy together. That home, in other words, fit my fantasy of what life with Justin *might* be like as opposed to what it really was. When I moved in, of course, the fantasy seemed as real as it ever had.

That first month or so, we had nothing to do but train and spend time together, and it was probably the best single period of our entire three-and-a-half-year relationship. We both focused equally on getting in shape for the coming season and on each other. During this brief period, the high drama that had defined our entire relationship disappeared. *Maybe,* I thought, *all that is now behind us. Maybe we've finally moved into the long-term-commitment and mutual-love-and-support phase of this once turbulent affair. I'm happy. He's happy. We're finally on our way.*

And then the season began.

THE 2006 TENNIS SEASON STARTED, AS USUAL, IN AUSTRALIA. I had entered the early-season tournament in Sydney to play doubles with Rennae Stubbs. Justin was there to practice for the week before the upcoming Australian Open in Melbourne

Rennae and I won our first round, but shortly after the match, I got sick with the stomach flu. Even so, she and I kept winning—so I tried to recuperate in my downtime and save all my energy for playing. In the semifinals, we were playing the #1 doubles team in the world at the time, Lisa Raymond (career doubles titles: 64) and Samantha Stosur. I was still struggling physically, but we were playing well. We eked out a victory in the third set, 6-4. I was both thoroughly exhausted and thrilled.

In the finals, we were set to play Virginia Ruano Pascual and Paola Suarez, another previously ranked #1 team. Due to rain delays, we ended up taking the court just before midnight. Justin had left for Melbourne by that time, after another series of petty arguments, but some wonderful pals had shown up to cheer us on, despite the weather and the late hour. Among them were Kristine Kunce, a good friend with whom I'd played doubles early in my career; and her husband, Damian. (Kristine had since retired and now lived in Sydney.) Also present were my childhood friends Mike and Bob Bryan, the #1 ranked men's doubles team at the time and eventual winners of all four Grand Slam doubles titles; along with their coach, David Macpherson, known to all as "Macca." The Bryan twins had lost a match that afternoon, yet they (and Macca) had stuck around for eight long hours to watch Rennae and me play. They knew this was a big moment for me and wanted to be there.

Rennae and I took the court, and we were on fire. We won the first set easily, 6-2, and were up in the second, 5-2, serving for the match, when we let our guard down. We lost our focus, and our counterparts suddenly found theirs. My partner and I began to blow a big lead, and we could feel the title slipping away from us. Great players can seize a moment of vulnerability on their opponents' part . . . and these were great players. Rennae and I lost eight games in a row, lost the second set, and were down 0-2 in the third. We had dug ourselves into a serious hole.

However these things happen—and it can be mysterious at times—we both finally regained our composure and rallied, not ready to lose without a fight. We dug deep, and our earlier form returned. We were back in the zone, and this time, we stayed there. We won the next six games in a row, taking the third set, 6-2. After slipping so far behind, it was a rush to come roaring back.

For the first time since I'd been diagnosed with leukemia almost five years earlier, I'd won another WTA title. If only for a brief moment, I was back on top. It gave me a tremendous sense of pride to accomplish things *after* my illness that I'd accomplished pre-illness. It was further evidence that the cancer hadn't defined my life, only interrupted it. While tennis was no longer my raison d'être, it still felt great to win, and win on my own terms.

Not only had Rennae and I won, which was a glorious feeling, we'd won against one of the best doubles teams in the world at that time. The irony behind this win was that my doubles partner and I had always had a contentious relationship—at times on the Tour, we'd gone months without speaking to each other. We made amends before this tournament, of course, but we both loved the fact that we never intended to play together again, let alone win a title. In all ways, it was a sweet victory.

Rennae and I finished the match just before 2 A.M., and I made sure in my victory speech to profusely thank the Bryan twins and Macca, among the others, for sticking with us to the end. Back at the hotel, Bob Bryan retired for the night, but the rest of us stayed up and celebrated.

With only an hour of sleep, I took off for Melbourne the next day, unfortunately without Rennae as my partner. I found another partner at the last minute (Sania Mirza, a great singles player), but I played poorly and we lost in the first round. I reunited with Justin, as planned, but after those rough moments in Sydney, much of the goodwill and romantic afterglow we'd built in our first month of living together had dissipated.

After Melbourne, we went our separate ways again, a constant in pro touring: Justin went on to play in some additional tournaments, and I went back to our home in Santa Monica. We didn't see each other for a while, and things grew incredibly strained. Again, I fell into a protracted state of emotional ambivalence. Part of me was ready to leave, like dozens of times before, but I couldn't. The stakes felt higher. I had moved in with him, and that made it even harder for me to contemplate leaving. In fact, I wondered if that was why I had moved in with him in the first place—I wanted it to work out so much that I needed it to be harder to leave. I felt weak and tortured. Weak because I couldn't walk away and tortured because I didn't *want* to walk away. I yearned for a return to those idyllic weeks we'd had not that long ago, but I was saddened by the turmoil that was occurring once again, and ashamed that I'd put myself right back in it. And I knew I had no one to blame but myself.

The only path forward that made sense to me at the time was to hang in there until things eventually got better again.

SINCE I DIDN'T HAVE A STEADY DOUBLES PARTNER, I only played a few tournaments in the spring, with no notable results. In early April, Rennae and I decided to partner again for an extended length of time. Our first tournament under this new pact was on Amelia Island, off the east coast of Florida, north of Jacksonville.

Driving up by myself in a rental car from my parents' place in Boca, I was on the main highway, I-95, about three hours into the five-hour drive. I was getting drowsy, so I started to scan the surroundings for a Starbucks. I took my eyes off the road for no more than a split second, and when I looked back, the traffic ahead had come to a dead stop. I swerved to avoid the cars in front of me and went crashing headfirst into a guardrail. Like most car accidents, it was over before it began. But one of my feet had gotten jammed against the floorboard in an awkward fashion. I felt a searing pain in my left foot, but mostly I was shaken by the seemingly instant calamity.

I made it to Amelia Island and had my foot checked. When nothing came up on the MRI, I decided to play anyway, with my foot heavily taped. I played through the pain . . . but I played poorly. Rennae and I lost in the first round at Amelia Island and then lost in the first round of the next tournament on the Tour in Charleston, South Carolina. After the Charleston tournament, I had my foot examined again and was diagnosed with a hairline fracture in my fifth metatarsal. The treatment: keep my foot in a boot for the next six weeks. No tennis for at least two months.

During those tennis-free weeks, Justin and I were home together in L.A. and decided to use the time to work on our relationship. We were home on May 17, the fifth anniversary of the day I'd received my diagnosis, and I braced myself for another intense emotional reaction. The occasion tended to bring forth many feelings and memories for me, some of which were quite painful. I'd lost some profound things that day, such as my innocence and my trust in the future, not to mention professional acumen that was forever compromised. Even though I was still measuring what I'd gained from the ordeal, I felt deeply grateful that I had both survived, and set out on my own self-defined course. Two close friends, Jeb and Nancy Barrows, would later dub May 17 as my "re-birthday."

On this particular re-birthday, the plan was for Lindsay to treat me to a day of pampering at a local spa followed by a quiet dinner at one of my favorite restaurants in Santa Monica. After the spa, Lindsay and I went back to the house to pick up Justin for dinner.

Waiting to surprise me were about 20 loving friends. I was in shock. When I saw Kim—who, like Lindsay, had been with me through this whole strange period—I lost it and sobbed on her shoulder. Everyone in the room was in some way connected to my illness and recovery: some of them, like David Egdes, my old agent, had known me when I was sick; others I never would have gotten to know had it not been for the cancer. And Justin, the consummate host, had organized the entire party, from getting the crowd to show up on time to serving up cupcakes from my favorite bakery. The fact that it was all taking place in our mutually beloved home made it even more special . . . it was a truly joyful surprise.

Not long after this, I traveled to Europe with Justin for the tournaments he was playing there. As was often the case in the past, I continued my vacillation between focusing on my career when I wasn't injured, and focusing on my personal life when I was. Unfortunately, in both cases, I left myself, and the issues I needed to address, out of the equation. Our relationship continued to deteriorate, old destructive patterns continued, and I finally came to the realization that things hadn't changed—and never would. I reached my breaking point.

For the first time, I was no longer angry or hurt. I was just incredibly sad. Deep down I knew that this was the beginning of the end—the *real* end.

MY FOOT HAD FINALLY HEALED TO THE POINT that I could start playing tennis full-time again. A few weeks later, at the U.S. Open, Justin and I stayed in separate quarters. Although we hadn't officially broken up, I knew that this was the next step. The thought of it made me sick to my stomach, and I was horribly depressed. When Mircea, Laura, and the kids came to New York for a few days, I was so grateful to have them there, if only for a day or two.

I lost the second round of the doubles match I played with Michaëlla Krajicek. And strangely enough, the highlight of the trip was the first-round loss I suffered in the mixed doubles with Mike Bryan. We were up against his twin brother, Bob, and Martina Navratilova—and it was an entertaining, well-played match in front of a packed stadium. Even though Mike and I lost, it was a nice, albeit brief, escape from the reality of my life off the court.

After Justin and I were both out of the tournament, we finally broke up. I told him that I was done; I was emotionally shattered, and I could no longer maintain the charade that things would change. He wanted to continue trying, but I was completely spent and told him so. There was no reason to go over all the issues again. We both knew the intricacies of how and why our relationship had crumbled. This was the end, and while it was heartbreaking and painful, I knew deep down that I wouldn't go back.

I felt isolated and absolutely devastated, at which point Lindsay once again came to my rescue. Because of injuries, she'd only played in a handful of tournaments in 2006, but she competed in the U.S. Open and was planning to head straight off to Bali after that to play singles. Seeing the state I was in, she asked me to play doubles with her there. She said that we could both play together—and stay together—at the Four Seasons Resort. Her attitude was: "Let's just get you out of here. You don't want to go home and deal with this yet. Just come to Bali with me." I think she feared that if I stayed around, I might get sucked back into my relationship with Justin like I had a hundred times before. Given my track record, it was an understandable concern.

So I went straight to Bali and leaned on my best friend for the next week or so. If I had to be miserable, I might as well be miserable at the Four Seasons on an exotic island. We saw the trip as much as a vacation as another stop on the Tour: we hung out at the beach; didn't practice all that much; and entered tournament play with a relaxed, playful attitude.

And we won the championship.

It was only the second title I'd won since being diagnosed with leukemia—the first being the tournament in Sydney with Rennae only eight months before—and the first title Lindsay and I had won since our many pre-cancerous victories in 2001. It was a small tournament but a big triumph, certainly for me. For one, it helped offset the guilt and sense of failure I felt about splitting with Justin. Second, only a few weeks later, Lindsay found out she was pregnant. It had been our last chance to play together, and we certainly made the best of the occasion.

Having always found my relationship with Justin "mind blowing," in her words, Lindsay decided that she couldn't get involved in it anymore. "The two of you together were so crazy," she told me recently. "Yet I felt so guilty that my best friend was getting hurt and hurt and hurt—and kept walking back into the situation, almost asking for it. You tried with every ounce you had to make it work. When it ended, I was so happy to be there to help you come out of it."

I came back from Bali and went straight to Florida to be with my family. I couldn't face reality. I had no place to live and dreaded the idea of moving yet again. I knew I had to go back and dismantle the home I'd barely settled into, and I knew that it would be painful.

When I got back to California, Kim and Oliver invited me to stay at their place for as long as necessary. Their friendship and support meant the world to me: From playing doubles together to my illness, comeback, divorce, move to California, and now breakup with Justin, Kim had been there for me—patient, kind, and steadfast. She and Oliver understood me and everything I'd been through, and they loved and encouraged me the whole time. I was incredibly grateful to them for their support throughout, and for opening their home to me during such a difficult time. I couldn't have asked for a better place to stay.

After living out of my suitcase for the next few months, I finally faced up to my living situation, or lack thereof, and began to hunt down a place in L.A. I was playing in Zurich, and after some online research, I found a place in Hermosa Beach that looked promising, but I was worried that it might be gone before I got back to check it out. Kim and Lindsay, anxious to see me out of Justin's house (and life), offered to look at the place together. They liked it, and after my okay, signed me up long-distance. In Linz, Austria, the tournament after Zurich, I made the finals, partnering with the Slovenian player Katarina Srebotnik. I was happy to be doing well on the court but anxious to get back and start over *off* the court.

The last step was moving out of Justin's place. I went to his house alone and packed up all my belongings by myself. The effort wasn't physically taxing, but I have to say that it was right up there with the hardest thing I ever had to do. It was incredibly sad, an inescapable acknowledgment that my personal life was at a crossroads—again. In terms of sheer emotional anguish, moving out of that house was on a par with getting divorced four years earlier.

In fact, it was a little harder. The guilt associated with the divorce had been agonizing, but I'd had an overriding sense that I was doing the right thing for both Andrew and me. With Justin, there was an emotional connection that was still alive—sometimes flickering, sometimes in full flame—and although it was my decision to end things, it felt as if someone were ripping my heart out of my chest. I had no choice, really; if I wanted to preserve my sanity, I had to get out. To avoid the inevitable long-term pain, I had to endure some serious short-term anguish.

After the movers had left my new apartment, I remember that I stood there, alone and devastated amidst the chaos of boxes and bags. I sank to the ground in my half-empty living room, curled up, and bawled my eyes out.

There were more than a few days immediately after this final split when I had to force myself out of bed and remind myself to breathe. I counted the days since our last conversation, hoping that enough time would pass for my foggy state of sadness and regret to lift. If being with Justin was like a drug habit, this was my withdrawal in detox. Despite my addiction to the highs and lows of our relationship, what made my "recovery" all the more wrenching and protracted was that I couldn't make sense of the whole situation. I couldn't reconcile the feelings of love I had for Justin with the feelings of isolation, loneliness, and shame I felt within our relationship. How could those exist side by side? If I was so hurt in the relationship, why did I stay in it? Yet now that I was out of it, the pain I was feeling was almost unbearable. On top of the heartbreak, I was feeling massive confusion.

I WOULD EVENTUALLY LEARN A LOT from my relationship with Justin—I'd come to appreciate the aspects of it that awakened positive feelings in me, while recognizing the unhealthy aspects, and work on not repeating the same detrimental patterns. I would eventually accept that blurring two states—love and unhealthy attachment—added to my confusion and almost pathological inability to walk away. I came to understand that love isn't supposed to, and doesn't, hurt. But at the time, the only thing I really knew for certain was this: it was over, finally. And in the same way I was compelled to redefine myself in the wake of the leukemia and the divorce, I needed to do so once again— or maybe truly for the first time.

• • • • • •

Chapter 10

THE FINAL MATCH

As I was emotionally withdrawing from my three-and-a-half-year relationship with Justin, something that took more energy and effort than I could have ever imagined, I realized that this would be the absolute worst time to withdraw from tennis as well. I'd toyed with the idea of retiring during the coming off-season, but after the breakup, I knew there was only so much change I could take.

Trying to breathe new life into my career, I committed to playing doubles with Rennae Stubbs the following year. It was time to rededicate myself, I decided, so I poured myself into training for the month of December. Despite injuries, partner switching, and the turmoil with Justin, I *had* managed to win two tournaments in 2006. I wasn't quite a has-been yet. Plus, the focus on training was a great distraction from my failed relationship. Once again, I used the physical pain to escape my considerable emotional pain.

My family was incredibly supportive through this period, helping me nurse my broken heart. After all we'd gone through over the last five years—from the leukemia to the divorce and now this—my relationship to my family, I realized, was stronger than ever. I was now on my own and independent of their decision making, but I still felt certain that they would support me no matter what I decided. At one point, my mother even told me she was proud of me and admired my strength. Those were words I'd heard during and after the cancer but never expected to hear after yet another failed relationship.

THE 2007 SEASON BEGAN, AND I HIT THE COURT with high hopes. For the first time in a long time, I wasn't dealing with an injury. I also had a partner I could count on, and I planned on playing a schedule that wouldn't exhaust me but would still give me plenty of chances to win. Unfortunately, the plan was misguided, as I soon found out.

Rennae and I played together in Sydney and Melbourne with dismal results. Despite all my hard work in December, my tennis was a disaster. She and I lost in the second round in Sydney and the first round at the Australian Open in Melbourne; we were nowhere near the form that had won us a title in Sydney exactly a year before. For whatever reason, things just didn't click. After our poor showing in Melbourne, we decided we were a doubles team that worked best only playing sporadically and not match after match. We decided to split up.

Doubles tennis involves more than two good players. Complementary playing styles; personalities that mesh; and, perhaps most important, chemistry, are all factors that make a great team. The really successful doubles teams—Martina Navratilova and Pam Shriver, for instance, or Bob and Mike Bryan—have great, intangible chemistry. In a high-speed doubles match, where instinct and synchronicity are everything, you and your partner have to play almost as one person, knowing what the other person is thinking while she's thinking it. Rennae and I didn't have that chemistry. We looked good on paper, and could even win on occasion through the combined skill of two veterans, but our personalities on the court didn't connect and we could never find a consistent rhythm in our game. The split was amicable; we both acknowledged the situation.

I was now completely partnerless, both on and off the court, for the first time since I was 15, when Andrew became my full-time coach and companion. My dad said the reason he chose to play tennis was because it's a sport where your destiny is in your own hands. However true that is in singles, it doesn't apply to doubles. No matter how hard you train or how skillful you become, you have to rely on someone else's commitment and performance to be successful. Your destiny is only 50 percent in your hands. Having looked for and found the right partner on many occasions, I knew how difficult it was, and at this point in my career, I was weary of trying to find yet another perfect match.

A big factor in all of this was the harsh reality that, to borrow a term from Wall Street, my stock in the tennis world was down. Way down. As with any professional sport, new players are popping up constantly—many from the far reaches of Russia and China—and they weren't exactly looking at me, a 29-year-old veteran, as a promising investment as a doubles partner. Most of these 18- and 19-year-olds probably didn't know that I had been ranked #1 in the world in the not-too-distant past and had won a fair number of big tournaments, Wimbledon included. They only knew my results from the last week or the week before, and those results weren't good.

It was difficult for me to come to terms with the state of my career. I knew that, post-cancer, I was operating with a whole new series of physical limitations. I knew that I wasn't the player I once was. I knew that I was gradually losing my edge—the egocentric, relentless, almost obsessive devotion to the game that winning on the highest level demanded. I knew all of that, at least intellectually. But emotionally, the feelings of inadequacy I'd felt so strongly in Auckland two years ago were creeping back in. I struggled to find partners, I wasn't playing well, and my ranking was dropping. Being faced with that reality week in and week out was challenging to deal with. The flip side was that I was afraid to step away, once again faced with the question: "What will I do next?" I was stuck between disappointment and fear.

IN FEBRUARY, I MADE WHAT I NOW CONSIDER TO BE the best decision of my life: I scheduled an appointment with a psychologist. I had returned from that disastrous trip to Australia, partnerless and demoralized, and I felt that my life was in a tailspin. Tennis had in no way compensated for the sadness and self-loathing I felt about my personal life. And it wasn't just the breakup with Justin that had me reeling—it was the fact that I'd spent three and a half years of my life in another unhealthy relationship. How could I have let that happen? What was wrong with me? If I thought I deserved better, why did I continue to settle for less? How could I willingly invite more turmoil into my life?

I'd focused all my off-court energy on "fixing" my relationship and little energy on turning inward and fixing myself. I could blame the whole confusing mess on my ex-boyfriend, but that wouldn't do anything to solve my problem. I had obviously contributed to the turmoil as much as he had, and I was now incredibly scared that I might turn around and put myself in the same situation. I didn't want to repeat the cycle. I finally hit bottom and accepted that I needed help.

Some people turn to drugs, alcohol, or other destructive behaviors to escape the pain in their lives—I'd obviously turned to a man. I had jumped into my relationship with Justin headfirst without addressing the issues that had haunted me for most of my life. I now understand why people recommend *not* getting involved in a relationship after a serious breakup or traumatic event. You need time by yourself, time to process everything. The leukemia had helped me get out of a dysfunctional marriage, grow out of the shadow of my parents, move to California, and get back to tennis on my own terms. Now, the extreme nature of my affair with Justin and the intense heartbreak I felt after our breakup was the catalyst to go further—to confront my own internal barriers to true independence.

A good friend of mine in L.A. had been through severe childhood trauma and had seen several therapists over the years. She's smart as a whip, so when she said she could recommend someone she really trusted and respected, I saw my opening and called Dr. Janine Shelby right away. During our first meeting, the very first thing I said to her was: "I need help." I don't think I'd ever spoken those words out loud in my entire life. It was such a relief to make that admission and realize everything it meant. With help, I knew I could address all of those personal issues that had led to my current tailspin and learn to recognize and combat the habits that had failed me over and over again.

I remember telling Raj about my revelation, and he reacted with an inquisitive look on his face. "Really?" he replied, almost disbelieving. "Well, good for you." He knew what a difficult, yet pivotal, step it was for me.

Feeling excited about committing to my psychological well-being, I decided to call my parents. I announced that I was seeing a therapist, and my dad's reaction—which I should have guessed before even picking up the phone—was: "Well, I guess everyone who lives in California needs a psychologist." My response was, "Yeah, Dad, either that or the people who have leukemia at age 23 and almost die—they might need a psychologist, too."

My mom then got on the phone, wondering if I was suicidal or dangerously depressed. I had to assure her that I wasn't about to jump off a bridge. I was seeing a therapist, not committing myself to a mental institution! I wasn't surprised by my parents' reactions, only slightly annoyed. In their view, one turned to faith and family to solve problems, not some expensive professional listener. I understood their Eastern European perspective—strong, stoic, and highly structured—I just didn't abide by it anymore.

Over the course of our work together, Dr. Shelby (soon just "Janine") gave me the strength and insight to listen to myself. Besides that brief meltdown in Auckland in 2005, ably attended to by my amateur-shrink-on-call at the time, Raj, I had never really faced up to my thoughts about myself. Thanks to Janine's strong recommendation that I write down my feelings—the same tool Raj had suggested two years before—I began to pay close attention to what was going on inside of me.

My one-dimensional upbringing, my illness, my divorce, my relationship with Justin, my parents, the whole business of tennis . . . for the first time, I began to deal with them all as one long and interconnected reality, not just small fires to be put out to get through the day. Even though I'd had a phoenix tattooed on me in 2005, I hadn't truly risen above or dealt with all of the challenges in my life. I didn't realize it at the time, but I was still mired in the ashes, struggling to extricate myself and make sense of my illness and the traumatic fallout.

What I began to realize over time was that each critical event in my life over the last six years had been a loss: loss of health, loss of innocence, loss of a marriage, loss of a serious relationship. And I was facing the impending loss of the main thing that had defined me since I was six years old: tennis. Although I'd fretted about, cried over, and tried to get past every one of these losses, what I hadn't really done was accept them and mourn their passing. I'd never *allowed* myself to mourn—the deep, sometimes confusing process of feeling the grief and pain of loss, and then putting it behind me.

There is no one right way to mourn—no right time or right duration—but there *is* a price to pay when one glibly decides to "get on" with life and bury those painful feelings. They keep coming back in a hundred ways. For me, they kept making me feel sad, guilty, vulnerable, and inadequate. Perhaps coming to grips with the fact that my tennis days were numbered allowed me to combine all the other losses into one cathartic act of mourning.

The other side of mourning, I came to see, was a renewed sense of my own worth, apart from all the things that had happened to me in the past. Clichéd as it might sound, I had to learn to love myself again—or perhaps love myself, truly, for the first time—independent of fathers, husbands, boyfriends, and tennis trophies. I could no longer rely on anyone else to validate me or tell me how I felt.

To help me with this process, Janine suggested that I bring in a photograph of myself as a child. I chose the one I mentioned earlier in this book, where I'm dressed in my little tennis outfit and off to play my very first tournament. I selected it because I thought it perfectly represented the scared little girl I often was in my childhood. Even at age six, I felt stress, tension, and fear. At the moment that photo was taken, it was all I could do not to throw up.

Janine asked me what I would say to that little girl. I started telling Janine, and she stopped me. "Tell *her*," she said. Somewhat reluctantly (old habits die hard), I did what Janine asked, and began speaking to that six-year-old child. The emotions became overwhelming. Through heaving sobs, I managed, "It's going to be okay. You don't have anything to be afraid of. I love you unconditionally. I will be here for you. And I will protect you."

My assignment from Janine was to continue talking to that little girl in the photo, and through that process, I hit upon a couple of key insights. One, it was time to pay attention to her and give her the personal love and support she felt was missing, and it was now *my* responsibility to do this—no one else's. Second, I realized that there was nothing to be scared of anymore. I was an adult, I could make my own decisions, and I wasn't in any imminent danger. The source of my fear was in my own head, not the outside world. I had spent my life up to this point relying on the judgments of other people to guide my way, from those of my father and coaches on the tennis court, to those of Andrew and Justin in my personal life.

Justin, I guess, was the last link in the chain. I was relying on him so much to make me feel worthy and loved after my illness, divorce, and struggling career that I kept making costly excuses for bad behavior. I felt that I'd failed at marriage, and I didn't want to fail at another relationship. He was also a link to the world of pro tennis. As much as part of me wanted to break away from the hermetic world of my sport, there was another part of me that wanted to stay in it for as long as possible. Like my last relationship, fights and all, it was familiar.

The process of detaching myself, and my self-worth, from the outside forces I'd relied on to provide my life direction and meaning took time. It was some of the hardest work I've ever done. And even though I was beginning to see tennis from a more detached point of view, I still wasn't ready to throw in the towel.

I CONTINUED PLAYING THAT SPRING with random partners, with no dramatic results. I'd decided to keep signing up for Tour events as both a distraction and a means of income while I was trying to put the pieces of my life back together. It gave me a sense of normalcy, since it was the one constant in my life.

I continued to see Janine as often as I could when I was back in Southern California, and we'd supplement our in-person meetings with phone sessions when I was on the road. Janine gave me "homework," and I no longer dismissed such introspective exercises the way I might have in the past. When Raj had told me to go back to my room in Auckland and write down my most intimate thoughts, I bitched and moaned and let the practice drop soon after the crisis had passed. Now it was my main job in life. Playing tennis became something I did between the ongoing work of straightening myself out, not the reverse.

As I focused on my internal issues over the course of the 2007 season, the fact that I wasn't winning on the court didn't affect me in the same devastating way it had in the past. It was a clear sign I was "getting over" tennis for the first time in my life.

I remember playing the tournament in Miami in late March, then sitting in my hotel room working on one of Janine's assignments. This one involved listing all of my most prevalent feelings, the reasons behind them, and then thinking about whether or not I wanted to hold on to them.

Here are three examples of what I wrote down that day:

Fear/Scared

- *worried about what others may think, worried about letting people down, comes from my need to please others*

- *most of my experiences with voicing my own needs/desires have been met with resistance and negativity*

- *afraid of falling into another unhealthy relationship*

- *afraid of failing*

Ashamed/Inadequate

- *embarrassed by the shortcomings of my career after my illness*

- *stems from all of my experiences with tennis and my self-worth always being measured by wins and losses*

Angry

- *felt abused and taken advantage of, somewhat betrayed by the people closest to me, maybe even by life in general?*

- *learning that it is okay to feel angry, must learn to feel it, accept it, deal with it in a healthy way*

Some of these emotional states served me well; others did not. The idea was to keep the ones from which I gained some benefit, and throw away the ones that had no positive purpose. I immediately dismissed the "Ashamed/Inadequate" entry, for instance, knowing that it served no other purpose than to make me feel bad about myself.

The "Angry" entry, on the other hand, was eye-opening. I realized at that moment that I was still enraged, below the surface, by the injustice of getting leukemia at 23 and seeing my once-promising tennis career ripped away from me. When I returned to competitive play, I carried that rage with me: I mildly resented all of the women around me and their successes—these healthy, thriving players I'd often beaten before the cancer, players I'd be facing at a particular tournament. That anger was useless, both on the court and off, but I'd never fully acknowledged it until I wrote it down.

During the time I had leukemia, I buried the anger because being pissed off wasn't part of the script I'd learned so well. The situation called for me to be superhuman, tough it out like a pro, and remain happy and upbeat throughout. After all, I was known for my "picture-perfect one-handed backhand" and my "sunny disposition." I knew that during and after my battle with leukemia, I had to maintain that cheerful manner to make the whole ordeal easier for everybody else.

Letting go of the anger over my career and my illness was easier than I thought. I'd been dealing with this on some level during the past six years, so finally getting the pain out into the open and acknowledging it was a relief. It was like the Auckland meltdown all over again. I'd taken a big step there in New Zealand two years ago, but it hadn't stuck. I fell back into old habits and patterns, one of those being my relationship with Justin. This time, however, I knew I wasn't going to fall back into my old destructive habits. I had an inner sense of strength I'd never felt before, and I knew that this time, it would absolutely stick. But, like my recovery from leukemia, the road wasn't easy.

Letting go of my anger toward Justin—and more important, the anger toward *myself* for staying with him—was a tougher process. What made it even more difficult was the fact that I continued to see my ex at tournaments, so I was constantly faced with old demons. While I tried to handle the situation in a mature way, it was a continual inner struggle.

By late April, I'd partnered back up with Patty Schnyder, someone I truly enjoyed playing with. We decided to play both the French and Wimbledon, so I went straight to Paris, avoiding the lead-up European tournaments, as I was now used to doing. But things got off to a rough start. I arrived with an awful cough and a terrible case of jet lag, and the weather was dismal. It was cold and rainy, making practice extremely unpleasant and causing delays in the schedule and difficulty getting practice times.

On top of all that, Justin was there and not speaking to me. My parents had come to watch me that year, and we were having dinner at a restaurant that Justin and his new girlfriend happened to be at as well. They were a table or two away, and I remember feeling a chill in the air. It was disconcerting, but it was part of the price of having once been in his life. It was also ironic how my family and Justin had completely switched roles in my life: in 2003, he was by my side while I was fighting with *them;* in 2007, they were by my side while I was dealing with the fallout of my breakup with *him.*

Patty and I eventually lost a heartbreaking three-hour match in the first round after waiting for days for the weather to clear. All in all, it was an emotional and stressful trip, and I couldn't wait to fly home.

After another quick loss at Wimbledon, I played a season of Team Tennis and then had to make a decision about the series of five tournaments leading up to the U.S. Open. Patty only wanted to play one of the lead-ups, which meant I had to find another partner for the others. At that point, Meghann Shaughnessy, another great American player, offered to team up to play the entire series, including the Open. I obviously loved playing with Patty, but I really needed continuity at that point. Plus, with the Olympics on the horizon, there was always a possibility that Meghann and I might contend for a spot representing the United States in Beijing. So Patty and I parted company, again, and Meghann and I set out to play a couple of lead-ups before heading to the big tournament at Flushing Meadows.

The Rogers Cup alternates between the cities of Montreal and Toronto, and that summer it was played in Toronto, which had always been one of my favorite stops on the Tour. I loved the city, I loved the tournament, and I was eager to test out my new partnership. My enthusiasm, unfortunately, began to wane quickly. For one thing, I was lonely. Meghann was incredibly sweet, but she kept to herself; Raj couldn't make it that week; and my best bud, Lindsay, was at home tending to her brand-new baby boy, Jagger.

Without close friendships, which I'd sought throughout my career, tennis can be a nomadic and isolating existence. This is even more the case on the women's Tour—for whatever reason, it lacks the easy camaraderie of the men's, something Justin discovered when he'd go to women's tournaments with me. "No one talks," he'd say, and he was right. Many female players turn pro at a much younger age than male players do, and they're often isolated by design, their competitive lives structured by overbearing parents or controlling male coaches. When you walk into a typical male players' lounge, you usually hear laughter. In the female players' lounge, you might hear an outraged parent complaining about practice times. Or sometimes nothing at all.

Of course, I had known this and lived with it since I had been one of those teenage players with the protective coach. But as I ordered room service and ate alone every night in Toronto, I felt especially isolated. Now 29, many of my friends were long gone from tennis and on to the next phase of their lives. I was spending more of my time working on myself—via the therapy I was doing with Janine—than working on my backhand. This work, which involved mourning the loss of many things, was a lonely process as well. My one respite from this isolation was yoga, something Janine had recommended earlier in the year and that I was slowly beginning to understand and appreciate. Since I had so much free time, I decided to try meditation as well. Every night in my room, I'd practice being still, beginning with only ten concentrated minutes at first. This was nothing earth-shattering, I knew, but I was taking baby steps. I didn't realize then that my baby steps would turn into a gigantic leap.

The same could not be said for my tennis scores. Yoga or no yoga, meditation or not, Meghann and I lost the first match in the first round we played together, not an auspicious start to our partnership. I went back to my hotel room that night, ordered room service, and began to contemplate my next move. And then it hit me:

I don't want to do this anymore.

This message was clear; unambiguous; and spoken without anger, regret, or tacit self-criticism. For the first time, I also knew it was the truth. I don't know if it was the meditation, the benefits of therapy, or the loneliness of that hotel room—but for the first time in my life, I actually sat still and tried to let myself go. I simply paid attention to what I was feeling beneath the hardened layers of fear, insecurity, and discomfort. I suddenly knew with every fiber of my being that I was done. It had nothing to do with the loss a few hours before. I just didn't want to live that life anymore. I didn't want to fly to another city, check into another hotel room, find another partner, and then win or lose. That lifestyle didn't bolster my identity or feed my soul. The sacrifices were too great, and the rewards were no longer worth it.

I suddenly didn't care that I didn't have another job lined up, let alone a new career. This was such a huge step for me. I'd spent my entire life making plans, trying to control every turn in the road, always needing to know my next move. There is an enviable structure to being a professional athlete. There's a hard-and-fast training schedule, then a touring schedule, then two weeks off, and then the start of the next training schedule. Before the leukemia, I could map out my life months, if not years, at a time. I could tell myself where I'd be and what I'd be doing on a Tuesday in June when it was still December. Now the future was just one blank calendar page. And I didn't care! I just knew I didn't want to play tennis anymore, and that was enough for me.

It was probably the most liberating moment of my life.

I CALLED ROBIN WHITE, A FRIEND AND FORMER PLAYER. She worked as a coach for the USTA and was already in New Haven, Connecticut, the site of the next tournament after Toronto. We agreed to get away from tennis briefly and take a day trip to New York. I remember being happier on that brief excursion than I'd been in years. I was free! Robin was the perfect person to be around just then. As an ex-player who'd never defined herself by what she did for a living, she understood exactly what I was feeling. This was unusual, believe me. In the past, most players would recoil in horror when I'd say that I was thinking about quitting. They'd ask, "Why would you want to give up this lifestyle when you've still got a few years left in you?" Nonplayers reacted in the same way. I often heard, "You should hang on and play for as long as you can. The real world sucks."

I knew I was living a privileged life, one that others either loved or envied, but I also knew that this life was no longer fulfilling or enjoyable for me. I was beyond allowing myself to be talked back into another season. Nothing anyone else said or did now would make any difference. I felt strong and completely, innately confident in my own decision.

Meghann and I played the tournament in New Haven and again lost in the first round. I decided then that the next tournament, which was the U.S. Open, would be my last. I only told the people closest to me, some of whom probably thought I'd have a change of heart before the end of the Open. Nevertheless, everyone was very supportive, including my father. In fact, he'd been counseling me to retire for the last couple years. How ironic is that? My dad, the driving force behind my entire tennis life, wanted me to stop, but I insisted on staying the course. It was a matter of doing things on my own time schedule and for my own reasons. Quitting when he wanted me to quit would be as bad as playing because he wanted me to play.

I decided not to tell Meghann my decision going into the Open, since I thought it would only make her feel more pressured to help me go out on top. We played our first round on an outside court against two scrappy players, Martina Müller and Gabriela Navratilova (no relation to Martina), and we were favored to win. We won the first set easily but stumbled badly in the second, losing 7-5. We were both upset and not communicating. My head started to spin. I knew this was my last U.S. Open, not to mention my last tournament, period, and I wasn't about to go out losing in the first round on an outside court. There was no way that was going to happen.

I was pissed off, and I always seemed to play better angry. I started the third and final set like a woman possessed. Something inside of me took over, and I turned in one of the most impressive performances of my entire career. Raj later called it "one of the most incredible displays" he'd ever seen from me. Meghann and I won handily, 6-1, and I walked off that court immensely proud of myself. If only I could have summoned that level of intensity in every match before I decided to retire!

Once Meghann and I had gotten the monkey off our backs with that first victory, we just clicked. We won the second round easily, and after that match, I told her my decision to quit. We weren't close friends, but we knew each other well enough that she understood the importance of this moment for me. She wanted to play well for me and make my last tournament a memorable one.

We had a very tough matchup in the third round, against a team (Gisela Dulko and Maria Elena Camerin) who had just beaten the #1 team in the world in the previous round. But Meghann and I came out on fire and never looked back. My partner played the best tennis she'd ever played alongside me, and I kept up the same intensity I had since round one. We won the match, 6-1, 6-2, and were headed toward the quarterfinals. This was the first time in 2007 that I'd won more than one round in a tournament. I was finally relaxed, unencumbered by performance anxiety, and it showed in my game. My blissful state of mind had *nothing* to do with tennis—it had *everything* to do with the internal harmony I felt as a result of the decision I'd just made. Only by deciding to stop playing could I play at the top of my game.

Meghann and I were now only three matches away from the title. Unfortunately, professional tennis is not a Hollywood movie, so the outcome is not assured. We played on the grandstand court, and our opponents were Kveta Peschke and—as the very small world of tennis would have it—my old partner, Rennae Stubbs. In short order, they beat us easily, 6-2, 6-2. We didn't particularly falter; they just played much, much better on that particular day. I didn't spend a lot of time post-match ruing the outcome. I was content with my play throughout the tournament, not to mention my decision to call it quits. I walked off the court with the biggest smile on my face. I quite possibly could have been the happiest loser in the history of tennis.

I had no interest in making my retirement a big media event, so I hadn't told the press or any of the officials at the WTA my decision beforehand. I simply wanted to be with the people closest to me. The first person I saw as I walked off the court, and immediately hugged to death, was Raj. For five of the toughest, most tumultuous years of my life, he'd stood by me at every turn, encouraging me, supporting me, suffering through my emotional tailspins, and always nudging me to both play better and treat myself better. I couldn't have asked for a better coach, or a better friend, for that period of my life and the last phase of my career.

While I was surrounded by other friends, including Robin (who'd come to watch me play my last tournament), Raj took off and returned with a bucket of ice and a bottle of champagne. A small group of us then retired to a courtyard outside the players' lounge and cracked open the bottle. We had a going-away party right there, and people I'd known for years walked by and wondered why we were throwing an impromptu party in the middle of the players' area. Once we told them the reason, they joined right in the celebration. Some brought more drinks, and others brought food to absorb the alcohol. It was the ideal retirement bash.

Finally, two members of the WTA communications staff wandered by. When they found out what was going on, they were upset that they hadn't been able to plan a bigger, splashier affair for my last hurrah. I was really glad that they didn't. This was the way I wanted to go out—quietly and among friends. The party continued well into the night with more eating and drinking at the swanky New York restaurant Buddha Bar, with lots of toasts and salutations to my late tennis career. It was a perfect way to celebrate the end of one chapter in my life and the beginning of the next.

Another coincidence in all of this was that Justin had decided to retire that same week at the same U.S. Open. After playing and losing to Andy Roddick in the first round at Arthur Ashe Stadium, he went out in a blaze of cameras and reporters.

I AWOKE THE NEXT MORNING IN AN ALMOST ALTERED STATE of consciousness. I realized that I would never again have to check a match schedule, book a practice court, or look at a draw to find my name. I would never again have to pick myself up after losing or bring myself down after winning. I would never again have to check the rankings to see where I stood and get frustrated that my "number" wasn't higher. I would never again be judged, or judge myself, by the errant bounce of a small yellow ball.

And it felt damn good.

Word gradually seeped out that I was calling it quits, and although there weren't any big headlines like the ones surrounding my leukemia episode, there were hundreds of warm fan letters and some very nice farewell remarks in the press.

For example, a month after my announcement, I played the annual WTT (World Team Tennis) benefit exhibition event for AIDS hosted by Billie Jean King and Elton John. I was playing with Andy Roddick (again) in a mixed doubles match, and this was how the ESPN Website reported it:

> Roddick and Morariu hammed it up during [the match]. At one
> point, they pretended to argue. Roddick stalked off in mock fury,
> then wheeled and yelled out: "I can't stay mad at you!"
> We understand why. Morariu, 29, is one of the most gracious,
> graceful performers in the game and her low-key, unannounced exit
> was typical of her modest personality. Morariu retired after this year's
> U.S. Open and said there will be no reversal of that decision.

I don't know about the other statements, although I do appreciate the compliments, but they definitely got one thing right: I never
once thought of changing my mind. I made a pact with myself to take
some time and not rush into another job or career path. I had no real
idea exactly what I wanted to do next, but then again, I had no real
fear that I would end up doing nothing but sit around telling tennis
stories. I was incredibly grateful for all that the game had given me—
the opportunity to travel the world, make lasting friendships, and challenge myself in ways I never could have otherwise. It also gave me the
luxury of easing my way into my next life. All those years of traveling
and playing had afforded me the financial freedom to take time off and
not stress about paying bills. I worked out when I wanted, not because
I had to for tennis, or because I was trying to run from something,
but simply because it felt good. I also spent my time reading, doing
yoga, going to the beach, and reconnecting with people outside the
insulated bubble of the tennis world.

I continued to see Janine and work through the drama and hard-
ships of my life, especially those of the last six years. I knew I'd reached
a new equilibrium, and a new appreciation for all I'd been given. I had
a whole new rapport with my family; dear and loyal friends; my health;
and probably the greatest gift of all—a new relationship with myself.
I knew that I would never again abuse that relationship or take it for
granted. It was, and is, the most important one of them all.

• • • • • •

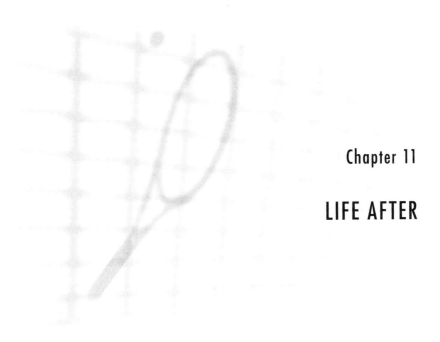

Chapter 11

LIFE AFTER

As things turned out, I never really left the world of tennis once I retired. As I took a breath to adjust to my new status as an ex-professional, I was asked by Tennis Channel to come aboard and provide commentary for a few tournaments in the fall of 2007. I immediately said yes, and I've been working for them ever since.

I've had a relationship with Tennis Channel since their inception. Along with Pete Sampras, I was one of the first two players they profiled in their half-hour, behind-the-scenes show, *No Strings*. It was about a year after I'd contracted leukemia and was fighting my way back to health. The program shows photos of me at my very worst during the chemo treatments—bald, weak, and sallow—and ends with the ceremony where I received the first Corina Morariu Courage Award. My mom appears throughout the program and conveys the horror and uncertainty of those cancer days better than I ever could.

I have really enjoyed broadcasting. Tennis Channel offered me a few opportunities to commentate while I was still playing, which gave me enough of a taste to know that I wanted to continue. Today, I appreciate the challenge of drawing the audience into the intricacies of the game. I also love the people I work with. The transition from being a tennis player to having a job in the "real world" can be a difficult one, in that one has to adjust to the more formal, structured demands of the corporate world, not to mention adjusting to reporting to someone else and not being one's own boss. Tennis Channel has made that transition seamless for me. They've been so wonderfully supportive that I truly feel like I'm part of a family rather than a company.

Having said that, going from playing to commentating was a difficult transition for me in another respect. The nature of tennis is completely objective: You win or you lose. You hit the ball inside the line or you don't. You have a number next to your name that clearly defines your standing. How well you do as a color commentator at a tennis match, on the other hand, is completely subjective: You're open to constant criticism. You'll have one fan saying that you're the best, followed by another saying, and I quote: "C'mon with the delivery already. You are not in the third grade and neither are the people listening to you. Pick it up, girlfriend."

Brickbats aside, going from the court to the broadcast booth was the perfect leap forward. I was forced to get over the fear of being a novice at something after a lifetime of mastering one particular skill. I had to focus on getting better at it and to learn to let go of what other people might think, good or bad. Again, working with Janine helped me enormously. Hearing harsh criticism still stings at times, and I still have the impulse to try to make everyone happy, but I take comfort in working hard and knowing that I'm doing the best I can. As Raj always said, that is the one thing I can control.

As fate would have it, Justin also began to work for Tennis Channel on a regular basis after he retired at the same U.S. Open. I might have had a learning curve for becoming an on-air personality, but he was a natural. He'd been "commentating" about the world of tennis in one way or another since he first joined the Tour—and although sometimes he talked his way right into a firestorm, no one ever accused him of being shy or boring. He loved talking to the world . . . but, unfortunately, he had no interest in talking to *me*. In fact, he refused to talk to me for some time. After ignoring me at the 2007 French Open, he basically ignored me again at the 2008 French, even though we were both working for Tennis Channel.

Despite the tension with my ex, I became increasingly comfortable in my new role in the world of tennis. I remember the moment this became crystal clear to me. In May 2008 I'd gone to Paris to cover the French Open for the first time as a commentator. This was also the first time I was going to a Grand Slam event as a retired player. On the first day of the tournament, I was riding the transport bus with all the other broadcasters on our way to the courts. I was studying the draw sheet (the schedule that lays out who plays whom in the opening rounds), and as I was reading it, I turned to Katrina Adams, also an ex-player turned broadcaster, and announced, "I'm so happy I never have to look at a Grand Slam draw again as a player and try to find my name! I do not miss that at all!"

This was an epiphany for me. I knew I never wanted to play again, but scanning that draw really brought it home. Especially at a Grand Slam, with all of the built-in drama and tension—just searching for your name on a list and hoping you landed a beatable opponent and not anyone named Williams was high anxiety. I could love and appreciate tennis even more now that I was in the stands and not on the court.

Everything in my life converged at the Australian Open early in 2009. For six weeks before I left for Melbourne, I had a recurring dream that Justin and I had reconciled, not romantically, but as friends. In the dream, the two of us talked quietly together and decided to let the past go and just appreciate our relationship for what it was and how it had contributed positively to our lives.

I discussed this with Janine. I explained to her that I truly enjoyed my new career, but this one source of tension tended to color every stop on the Tour. Both consciously and unconsciously, I felt the need to make an effort to straighten things out with Justin.

I arrived in Melbourne for the Open, and while I was waiting in our production office for our first meeting to start, Justin walked in. My back was to him, so I turned to say hello. He came right up to me, and before I could speak, he said, in a very sweet way, "Hey, Corina, how are you?" And then he gave me a hug and a kiss. It was as if we were greeting each other in the normal course of our lives before we'd ever become romantically entangled. The exchange of pleasantries that followed was not the least bit loaded or fraught with subliminal anger or regret.

Toward the end of the second week of the tournament, Larry Meyers, the head of production for Tennis Channel, called me to say there was an idea floating around that Justin and I should call a match together. Knowing our history, he wanted to make sure I was okay with this. Without hesitation, I said that I was. Soon Justin and I were side by side, calling a late-round doubles match that happened to feature our old and dear friends Mike and Bob Bryan. Justin did the play-by-play, I did the color commentary, and we had a blast. We joked, we laughed, we described and analyzed. It was all good.

Afterward, we stopped to have a short, private chat. Justin was very forthcoming. He said, "I'm so happy that things are okay with us again. I wish I could have handled the situation differently, but I just didn't know how to deal with it. I did the best I could."

I looked at him and said, "I know."

And that was it. For the first time, I didn't feel the need to rehash anything in the past, to even any scores, or get in any last digs. The best part was that I'd already forgiven him—and most important, myself—before he'd even said a word. I'd already let go of all the sorrow and regret, but only at that moment did this become apparent to me.

I then told Justin about the book I was about to write, and he was incredibly supportive. He encouraged me to be honest about my experiences, while complimenting me on the way I handled them.

If that wasn't enough of an emotional denouement for one tennis tournament, I also decided to reconnect with my ex-husband, Andrew. We hadn't spoken much since the divorce, but since he lived in Melbourne, I simply sent him a text message asking if we could get together. We met for coffee one afternoon and talked without dredging up the past for the first time since the divorce. That was then. This was a whole new day.

• • • • • •

AFTERWORD

The way I see things now, contracting leukemia on a spring day in 2001 ended my quest for tennis greatness, but it was an extraordinary wake-up call for the rest of my life. I ended up surviving the cancer, of course, and learning something profound about myself in the process. But the total disruption of my carefully structured life set off a cascade of changes that took me all of the last eight years, and a lot of tears, to work through. As brutal as those years often were—bringing with them the physical debilitation caused by my illness, my divorce, the long schism with my family, the turmoil with Justin, and my coming to terms with my tennis career—they reshaped my life in ways I could never have imagined or planned for. The leukemia remade me. I did a lot of the work, of course, but the leukemia was the catalyst for the whole crazy journey.

My lovely collaborator on this book, Allen Rucker, asked me at one point in this process what I thought I was meant to be doing. My answer was simple: this. I'm doing exactly what I'm supposed to be doing, and my life is unfolding as it should. I'm learning, growing, falling, getting back up, dusting myself off, and moving forward. Broadcasting and writing this book feel as close to my authentic self as I've gotten so far. I'm making progress. I continue to make mistakes, but I've realized that you can't live, or learn, without them. Mistakes are not failures; they're opportunities. Opportunities to pause, look inside, evaluate, and do better next time.

It took me years to get to this point, but I also realize now that everything that has happened in my life has been a true blessing. It was a blessing that my parents taught me at a very young age to reach high and to acquire the discipline and strength of mind that helped me deal with my illness. It was a blessing that Andrew supported me and helped me develop as a player during those crucial teenage years. It was a blessing that I got a wake-up call at age 23 by being diagnosed with leukemia, surviving it, and gaining perspective and insight, not to mention the strength to change my life. It was a blessing that I accomplished so much in tennis before I got sick, not to mention all the dear friends I made along the way. And it was even a blessing that I loved, fought with, and finally reconciled with Justin.

I'm not being Pollyannaish here, although I still like to make everyone around me feel good. I'm simply being truthful. And I don't think I'm alone in feeling that a horrible event like cancer can end up giving much more than it takes away.

We're all afraid of suffering, but we're especially afraid that we'll be destroyed by it, that we won't have the will or courage or optimism to recover and go on with our lives. If my story has any value, I hope it is to let people know that this doesn't have to be the case. We are all stronger than we think. We all have the ability to face life's adversities and reinvent ourselves. Sometimes we have to be broken down in order to open up. By no means do I want to tell anyone how to deal with the challenges of life. I simply want to share my experience and what helped me along the way, with the hope that we can all gain strength from each other.

And don't worry, Dad, I long ago dismissed the idea that I had the brain of a chicken. It turns out that I have learned a great deal from the brain and the heart and the spirit of the two people who mean the most to me: you and Mom. I am incredibly proud to be your daughter.

• • • • • •

ACKNOWLEDGMENTS

First of all, I have to thank my family. Despite our occasional differences, I know how lucky I am to have your love and support. I love you all dearly. Dad, your strength, generosity, and willingness to sacrifice in order to make a better life for your family never cease to amaze me. I have learned so much from you, and again, I'm so proud to be your daughter. Mom, your wisdom, kindness, unconditional love, and optimism are a constant inspiration. If I'm lucky enough to have kids one day, I hope I can at least be half as good of a mother to them as you've been to me. I've been incredibly fortunate to have you as a role model, mom, and friend. Mircea, thank you for being my friend, my protector, my knight in shining armor, and the best big brother I could have ever asked for. Laura, you are part of our family, and I didn't know how much I would appreciate that when Mircea asked you to marry him. I not only have a sister-in-law whom I love, but a dear friend as well. Collin and Chet, I love you both more than words could ever possibly say. Watching you two grow up has been more fun than I could have imagined; and I've thoroughly enjoyed seeing the sweet, sensitive, well-mannered boys you've become. I am so proud of both of you.

Lindsay, I don't even know where to start. You've lived most of this book with me, and your friendship means more to me than words could ever express. Thank you for your love, loyalty, and support, and for being like a sister to me. Kim, you've been there for me every step along the way as well; and your kindness, patience, and honesty (not to mention your dancing skills) make me incredibly grateful to be your friend. Raj, I could not have asked for a better coach, friend, and mentor. You coached me in tennis, but more important, you coached me in life. Thank you for accepting me the way I am, while still pushing me to do and be better.

So many other friends and loved ones in my life—Robin, Jeb, Nancy, Simone, Binder (& Co), Ian, Troll, Billie Jean, Dave and Dominique W, Merk, Marla, Zanda, Radu, Dan, Katia, and the list goes on—I'm sorry I can't address you all individually, but I want you to know how grateful I am for each and every one of you and for what you bring to my life. Janine, thank you for working with me and helping me become a better person. Your insight and guidance have been irreplaceable.

To Dr. Goodman and all the other doctors and nurses at Jackson Memorial Hospital, a simple thank-you doesn't even come close to conveying my gratitude. You helped save my life, and I will forever be indebted to you for the care you gave me. To everyone at Tennis Channel—Larry, Bob, David, Ken, Brad, Leif, Rossi, and countless others—thank you for making work fun every single day. And thank you for your support, encouragement, and belief in me as I learned the ropes of an entirely new career.

Jill Kramer, this book would not have been possible without you, and words cannot express how much I appreciate the opportunity you gave me to tell my story. Shannon and everyone else at Hay House, working with you has been an absolute pleasure; and I know how lucky I am to have such a supportive, encouraging publishing company behind me. Allen, you started as my collaborator, but you have become my dear friend. I have drawn tremendous inspiration from you and your courage through adversity. You brought this book to life, and I thank you for your patience and encouragement throughout this process.

Ryan, everything in this book prepared me for meeting you. You have made my dream of a safe, healthy, loving, supportive relationship a reality, and I will always thank you for that. I love you.

• • • • • •

Corina, Lindsay, and me [center]
at tennis camp in Maui.

A NOTE FROM THE EDITOR

It's funny how one idle comment can be the impetus for something really amazing, and that's what happened in the fall of 2008. I was attending a tennis fantasy camp in Maui; and the celebrity pros were Corina Morariu, Lindsay Davenport, and Tom Gullikson.

On the last day of the camp, I was on a court with Corina and three other "campers," and Corina was patiently trying to correct a chronic problem with my forehand. I wasn't a very good student, so we just decided to go over to the side of the court and have some ice water (it was a sweltering day).

Corina happened to ask me what I did for a living, and I responded, "I'm the editorial director for a book publishing company in Carlsbad, California."

Corina thoughtfully replied, "I've been thinking about writing a book . . ."

I stared at her in wonderment, and exclaimed, "Oh my gosh, Corina. Your story would be perfect for Hay House!"

Fast-forward about three weeks (and I do mean "fast!") . . . and a contract had been signed, and Corina's book was in the works.

Some things are just meant to be.

Now, if I could only fix that unfortunate forehand slice of mine!

— **Jill Kramer**

ABOUT THE AUTHORS

Corina Morariu was ranked a career high of #29 in the world in singles and #1 in the world in doubles on the WTA Tour. She won the women's doubles title at Wimbledon in 1999 and the mixed doubles title at the 2001 Australian Open, reaching the Australian Open women's doubles final in 2005. In 2001, Corina was diagnosed with leukemia and underwent chemotherapy. She made a full recovery and returned to competition in 2002, later becoming the WTA Comeback Player of the Year. Her bravery during her illness, and her moving and inspirational story, continue to motivate players and fans throughout the world. Corina currently serves as a commentator for Tennis Channel.

• • •

Allen Rucker is the author or co-author of 11 books, including his memoir, *The Best Seat in the House: How I Woke Up One Tuesday and Was Paralyzed for Life.* He is also an award-winning TV writer and lives in L.A.

• • • • • •

We hope you enjoyed this Hay House book. If you'd like to receive our online catalog featuring additional information on Hay House books and products, or if you'd like to find out more about the Hay Foundation, please contact:

Hay House, Inc., P.O. Box 5100, Carlsbad, CA 92018-5100

(760) 431-7695 or **(800) 654-5126**
(760) 431-6948 (fax) or **(800) 650-5115 (fax)**
www.hayhouse.com® • **www.hayfoundation.org**

• • •

Published and distributed in Australia by:
Hay House Australia Pty. Ltd., 18/36 Ralph St., Alexandria NSW 2015
Phone: 612-9669-4299 • *Fax:* 612-9669-4144 • www.hayhouse.com.au

Published and distributed in the United Kingdom by:
Hay House UK, Ltd., 292B Kensal Rd., London W10 5BE • *Phone:*
44-20-8962-1230 • *Fax:* 44-20-8962-1239 • www.hayhouse.co.uk

Published and distributed in the Republic of South Africa by:
Hay House SA (Pty), Ltd., P.O. Box 990, Witkoppen 2068 • *Phone/Fax:*
27-11-467-8904 • info@hayhouse.co.za • www.hayhouse.co.za

Published in India by: Hay House Publishers India,
Muskaan Complex, Plot No. 3, B-2, Vasant Kunj, New Delhi 110 070
Phone: 91-11-4176-1620 • *Fax:* 91-11-4176-1630 • www.hayhouse.co.in

Distributed in Canada by:
Raincoast, 9050 Shaughnessy St., Vancouver, B.C. V6P 6E5
Phone: (604) 323-7100 • *Fax:* (604) 323-2600 • www.raincoast.com

• • •

Take Your Soul on a Vacation

Visit **www.HealYourLife.com**® to regroup, recharge,
and reconnect with your own magnificence. Featuring blogs, mind-body-spirit news, and life-changing wisdom from Louise Hay and friends.

Visit **www.HealYourLife.com** today!

HEAL YOUR LIFE ♥

Take Your Soul on a Vacation

Get your daily dose of inspiration today at **www.HealYourLife.com®**. Brimming with all of the necessary elements to ease your mind and educate your soul, this Website will become the foundation from which you'll start each day. This essential site delivers the latest in mind, body, and spirit news and real-time content from your favorite Hay House authors.

Make It Your Home Page Today!

www.HealYourLife.com®